Gnostic John the Baptizer:

Selections from the Mandæan John-Book

Together with Studies on John and Christian Origins, the Slavonic Josephus' Account of John and Jesus, and John and the Fourth Gospel Proem.

G. R. S. Mead

ISBN 1-56459-375-4

Kessinger Publishing's
Rare Mystical Reprints

THOUSANDS OF SCARCE BOOKS ON THESE AND OTHER SUBJECTS:

Freemasonry * Akashic * Alchemy * Alternative Health * Ancient Civilizations * Anthroposophy * Astrology * Astronomy * Aura * Bible Study * Cabalah * Cartomancy * Chakras * Clairvoyance * Comparative Religions * Divination * Druids * Eastern Thought * Egyptology * Esoterism * Essenes * Etheric * ESP * Gnosticism * Great White Brotherhood * Hermetics * Kabalah * Karma * Knights Templar * Kundalini * Magic * Meditation * Mediumship * Mesmerism * Metaphysics * Mithraism * Mystery Schools * Mysticism * Mythology * Numerology * Occultism * Palmistry * Pantheism * Parapsychology * Philosophy * Prosperity * Psychokinesis * Psychology * Pyramids * Qabalah * Reincarnation * Rosicrucian * Sacred Geometry * Secret Rituals * Secret Societies * Spiritism * Symbolism * Tarot * Telepathy * Theosophy * Transcendentalism * Upanishads * Vedanta * Wisdom * Yoga * *Plus Much More!*

DOWNLOAD A FREE CATALOG AT:
www.kessinger.net

OR EMAIL US AT:
books@kessinger.net

CONTENTS.

	PAGE
FOREWORD	v
I. JOHN THE BAPTIZER AND CHRISTIAN ORIGINS	1-28
A Recent Study on John's Symbolism	1
The John-passage in 'The Antiquities' of Josephus	2
The N. T. Account: The Dress and Food of Repentance	4
Popular Messianic Expectations	7
The Sanctification of the Jordan-water	9
The Probable Symbolic Signification of John's Baptism	10
The Baptism of the Proselytes	11
One of John's Discourses and its Symbolism	13
The Fish and Fishers Symbolism	14
Ḥani-Ōannēs-Iōannēs	16
John-Jonah	18
Rabbinic Fish Symbolism	20
The Samaritan Ta'eb: A Reborn Joshua or Noah	21
John's Eschatological Symbolism	22
John and Jesus generally	24
John and the Messiahship of Jesus	26
II. FROM THE JOHN-BOOK OF THE MANDÆANS	29-96
Introductory	29
i. THE GNOSTIC JOHN THE BAPTIZER	25-61
Portents at John's Birth	35
John's Proclamation concerning himself	40
His Assumption of the Prophet's Mantle	41
John's Light-ship	42
John the Ascetic	44
Of Judgment-Day	45
The Letter of Truth	46
John's Invulnerability	48
John and the Baptism of Jesus	48
John's Marriage	52
John on his own Passing	54
John's Birth, Upbringing and First Appearance	56
John's Answer to Jesus Concerning the Angel of Death	59

		PAGE
ii.	THE STORY OF THE BREACH WITH JUDAISM	62-70
	Miryai is expelled from Jewry	62
	A Variant of the Same	64
	The Exiled Community settle on the Euphrates	65
	The Jews persecute the Mandæans	67
	They beg them to Return	67
iii.	SOME TYPICAL EXTRACTS	71-96
	The 'Fisher of Souls' Saga	71
	The Light-ship of the Fisher	75
	The Good Fisher overwhelms the Evil Fishers	76
	The Final Submission of the Evil Fishers	79
	The Good Shepherd	81
	The Loving Shepherds of the Good Shepherd	83
	The Treasury of Life	86
	In the Beginning	89
	Exhortations	91
	The Song of the Poor's Exaltation	93

III. THE SLAVONIC JOSEPHUS' ACCOUNT OF THE BAPTIST AND JESUS — 97-119

INTRODUCTORY — 97

TRANSLATION OF THE INTERPOLATIONS — 103-110

i.	John's Proclamation and his Rebuke of the Authorities	103
ii.	His Interpretation of Philip's Dream	105
iii.	His Persistent Rebuking of Agrippa and his Execution	105
iv.	The Ministry, Trial and Crucifixion of Jesus	106
v.	The Treatment of the First Christians	107
vi.	The Trilingual Inscription concerning Jesus	108
vii.	Portents at the Death of Jesus and Rumours of his Resurrection	109
viii.	A Prophecy concerning Jesus	110

GENERAL REMARKS — 110

IV. THE FOURTH GOSPEL PROEM — 120-127

A NEW VERSION VENTURE — 120-127

Connection — 120
Translation — 123

AFTERWORD — 128

FOREWORD.

THE main materials contained in these pages will certainly be new for the vast majority of readers. Moreover the Mandæan narratives, legends and discourses are not only interesting because of their own distinctive matter and manner, but they are also arresting; for they raise a number of problems, some of which are far-reaching and one is fraught with implications of immense importance. The definite solutions of these problems, however, lie in the future, and the most important of them will perhaps never be reached; for, in the absence of straightforward historical information, general agreement on any subject that concerns Christian origins immediately or even indirectly is now well-nigh a psychological impossibility.

The writer's intention in publishing these selections is not to speculate about the problems, for we are not yet in a position to state them with sufficient accuracy, but the very modest undertaking of making accessible for English readers some specimens of narrative and doctrine from one collection only of the traditional gnostic material which the Mandæan scribes have preserved to our own day through centuries of copying, and which hands on an early literature purporting at least in part to go back to times contemporaneous with Christian origins. For I think it will be of service for them, as a beginning, to read for themselves what the Mandæans have conserved from the past of the now legendary story of their great prophet, John the Baptizer, and some of the most characteristic notions and doctrines ascribed directly to him,—and that too in their full native setting and not in the form of brief summaries or isolated sentences, which is practically all they will meet with in the very few articles on the subject which have yet appeared in English,—and in articles only, for of books there are none.

Moreover it has been impossible to do even this previously;

for it is only quite recently that we have had put into our hands a reliable and complete version in German of two of the three main collections preserved to us; and we are still awaiting the translation of the most important deposit, without which it is impossible to survey the whole field thoroughly and so make really reliable inferences. All prior attempts at partial translation have been tentative at best and for the most part erroneous. But though we are still without a scientific version of the Treasury, it is nevertheless already possible to give almost a complete setting forth of one topic; for the selections from the John-Book here presented include practically all the matter that refers directly to the prophet, seeing that the Treasury makes only one brief reference immediately to him.

In this material a figure is depicted which in many ways differs greatly from the familiar picture sketched in the gospels and briefly referred to in the classical Josephus. The interest of the Gnostics has never been in external history, so that for the most part we are either in complete ignorance of, or lamentably uninformed about, the persons of their great teachers and writers. Their interest was rather in inner or psychic story and the imaginative history of ideas. Consequently the Mandæan picture of John is the prophetical and intimate aspect it presented to those within the mystic atmosphere of the community and to the fond memory of an esoteric tradition. No external view is preserved. I have deliberately brought out this contrast as strongly as possible by setting the Mandæan story in the midst between two studies of traditions which make much of John's wild appearance and strange dress, a popular external element which would at first sight suggest an equally primitive quality of his thought and action. This has been done to enable the reader to realize as strongly as possible the difficulties surrounding the fundamental problem of historicity, though the sharpness of the contrast is already somewhat modified by the doctrinal considerations brought out in the first study, which may theoretically help to bridge over to some extent the gap between the crudest features of the popular external tradition and what claims to be an internal tradition, no matter how it may have been sublimated in the form in which it has reached us. The second study, on the Slavonic Josephus' account of the Baptist and Jesus, though throwing no, or scarcely any, light on doctrine, is, in my opinion, of importance from the point of view of possible external popular tradition, and in any case will be a novelty for most readers.

It is a remarkable and somewhat saddening reflection that now, when after long years of waiting we are at last obtaining adequate versions of these so faithfully preserved Mandæan gnostic scriptures, their handers-on themselves are dying out, and those of them who remain do not seem to be sufficiently instructed or to possess the general education to throw light on the problems which their documents present to scholars. They do not seem to have any notion of the history of religion or the critical power in any way to analyze their own scriptures and compare them with parallel developments in the past. What I do not quite understand, however, is why, with regard to the philological side of the subject, no attempt, as far as I can ascertain, has been made by any European Semitic scholar scientifically to study Mandæan with the Mandæans themselves, and so collaborate with them in translation. They all speak Arabic as well as their native tongue; and it is somewhat puzzling that neither Brandt nor Lidzbarski, who have, after the pioneer work of Nöldeke on the language, busied themselves so sedulously with the documents, should not have visited them. They are accessible; and indeed do not seem in any way to be averse from giving information, as is seen from Siouffi's informant in the eighties of last century and quite recently from the account of Miss E. S. Stephens (now Mrs. Drower). The latter has made great friends with the Amara community and gives an entertaining chapter about them, under the heading 'A Peculiar People,' in her brightly-written travel-book, *By Tigris and Euphrates*.¹ It is the description of an intelligent and deeply interested observer, but of one unacquainted with the literature of the subject, and therefore not in a position to press for information on points of importance, if perchance it could be obtained. The account deals with externals, but it may be of interest to our readers to reproduce what Mrs. Drower was told about the *shalmono* and the *masseqtā*-ceremony, or rite of the making of a 'perfect' in this connection.

"There is a way . . . in which a Subba may reach a state

¹ London, Hurst & Blackett, 1923, pp. 204-219.

of holiness akin to that of the dweller in Mshuni-Koshto [the M. Abode of the Blessed], and this strange and unworldly people often resort to it. To achieve this state a man must renounce worldly desires and the delights of the flesh, but his path is harder than that of the Catholic monk in that he continues to live among men, a layman, and amongst his family without being able to partake of the joys of family life. In fact, after the ceremony of renunciation has taken place, the funeral service is read over him and he is, henceforth, no more than a living ghost.

"He may carry on his trade of farmer, boat-builder, or silversmith as before; but his personal life is one of renunciation, deprivation and self-mortification. He may not smoke, drink wine, coffee, tea, or any drug. He may not give an order, or express a desire. Should he need anything, he must procure it himself, or do without. His detachment from worldly things must be so complete that if a fire were to burn his house, destroy his goods and suffocate his wife and children he must show or feel no trace of emotion. . . . 'A permanent gaiety must be shown in his face.'

"The ceremony which separates the 'shalmono' from the world of the living is called the 'Massakhto.' The applicant goes to the bishop, who questions him closely as to the seriousness of his intentions, and impresses upon him the irrevocable nature of the step he wishes to take. After seven days' preparation with the bishop, if the applicant's desire is unshaken, he spends seven days and seven nights in a church [?] or place apart.

"Every day the bishop and priests come to him, and for food the postulant eats three tiny flat loaves of sacramental bread, about as large as an Osborne biscuit, daily; also part of the flesh of a dove. . . .

"At the end of the week a feast is prepared to which the new 'shalmono' is invited, usually in the house of the bishop. At the end of the feast all the priests who have eaten arise, with a last mouthful of food in their hands. Solemnly, then, the Prayer for the Dead is recited for the 'shalmono,' and, just as for a dead man, the last mouthful is eaten, the last mouthful which is supposed to stay the departed soul on its journey through purgatory. . . .

"The life of a 'shalmono' is harder than that of a priest, for priests and priestesses may marry; indeed, marriage is obligatory."

The last sentence suggests that the *shalmono* is a celibate from the start, but Mrs. Drower has already spoken of his wife and children and quotes Siouffi to the same effect, and the documents lay it down expressly that celibacy in no case whatever was approved, not even in that of a prophet.

It is evident that we have in this indication of a present-day class of 'perfect' separated out from the mass of the faithful, a subject for sympathetic enquiry, with the object of ascertaining whether among them there are any who enjoy mystic experience, and if so what is its nature, and whether it throws any light on the spiritual phases of the tradition.

Mrs. Drower is happy in choosing for the heading of her account 'A Peculiar People' and not 'A Strange Sect' or some such title. For one of the great points of interest is that the Mandæans show all the signs of being a race distinct from their neighbours. They make no converts and seem for many centuries to have kept themselves to themselves. They are not Arabs or Jews in type, but (?) 'Babylonians,' 'Chaldeans,'—a problem for the ethnologist to decide.

I.

JOHN THE BAPTIZER AND CHRISTIAN ORIGINS.

A Recent Study on John's Symbolism.

A DISTINCT ray of light has been cast on the obscure background of Christian origins by Dr. Robert Eisler in a series of detailed studies on the movement and doctrines of John the Baptizer. These studies, with other cognate essays, appeared originally in the pages of *The Quest* (1909-14), and are now available in book-form in an arresting volume, called *Orpheus—the Fisher: Comparative Studies in Orphic and Christian Cult Symbolism*.[1]

By way of introduction and as the most complete contrast to the Mandæan tradition of the Gnostic John, I will set forth in my own way the chief points of these detailed and fully-documented essays in summary fashion. Eisler's main point of view is that John based his doctrines and practices largely, if not entirely, on the Hebrew scriptures—the Law and the Prophets —of which, he contends, he was a profound knower. The John-movement is thus regarded as a characteristic Jewish prophetical reform founded on absolute faith in the present fulfilment of prior prophecy. Hereby is brought out in the strongest possible manner the Jewish conditioning of John's preaching and teaching, and this stands in the sharpest contradiction to the

[1] London, Watkins, 1921. Chh. xv.-xxvi. (pp. 129-207) are devoted to the special subject of John and his doctrines.

Mandæan tradition which claims that John was a Gnostic and not a Torah-man, and declares that the Jews could by no means understand him, but on the contrary rejected his revelation and drove out his community.

In Eisler we have a ripe scholar in whom the heredity of Rabbinical lore is so to say innate. He has almost an uncanny *flair* for biblical texts; it is not too much to say that his knowledge of the religious literature of his people is profound, his acquaintance with oriental sources very extensive and his linguistic accomplishments are enviable. Few are thus better able to enter with sympathy and understanding into the idiosyncrasies and depths of the Jewish mind in the various periods of its development, and thus for the time to live in the prophetical, apocalyptic and rabbinical thought-world of the days of the Baptist and share in its old-time beliefs and hopes and fears. Our exponent is thus an excellent advocate of the theme he sets forth. If his wide-flung net has not caught all the fish of the literary and archæological ocean, he has fished most carefully the stream of John the Baptist tradition, apart from the Mandæan, landed a rich catch and shown others how most fruitfully to set about bringing to the surface things about John which have long been hidden in the depths of a buried past.

THE JOHN-PASSAGE IN 'THE ANTIQUITIES' OF JOSEPHUS.

In all reason, apart from Christian testimony, John the Baptizer is a historic character, witnessed to by the Jewish historian Josephus, the courtly Flavian chronicler who flourished in the last quarter of the

1st century A.D. The famous passage in his *Antiquities* (XVIII. v. 2, ed. Niese, iv. 161, 162) referring to John is undoubtedly genuine, and has been assailed only by the very extreme doctrinaire non-historical school, who find it a very inconvenient thorn in their flesh. A Christian forger would have dotted the i's and crossed the t's with the pen of his tradition, or at any rate betrayed himself in some way by the prejudice of his thought; but this we do not find. The passage runs as follows as nearly as I can render it:

> Some of the Jews thought that Herod's army had been destroyed, and indeed by the very just vengeance of God, in return for [his putting to death of] John the Baptizer. For in fact Herod put the latter to death [though he was] a good man, nay even one who bade the Jews cultivate virtue and, by the practice of righteousness in their dealings with one another and of piety to God, gather together for baptism. For thus in sooth [John thought] the dipping (in water) would seem acceptable to him (God), not if they used it as a begging-off in respect to certain sins, but for purity of body, in as much as indeed the soul had already been purified by righteousness.
>
> Now since the others[1] were gathering themselves together (or becoming organized),—for indeed they were delighted beyond measure at the hearing of his (John's) 'sayings' (*logoi*),—Herod, fearing that his extraordinary power of persuading men might lead to a revolt, for they seemed likely in all things to act according to his advice, judged it better, before anything of a revolutionary nature should eventuate from him, to arrest him first and make away with him, rather than when the change came, he should regret being faced with it.
>
> Accordingly, on Herod's suspicion, he was sent in bonds to Machærus,[2] the above-mentioned fortress, and put to death there. The Jews, however, believed that destruction befell the army to avenge him, God willing to afflict Herod.

[1] The rest of the Jews other than Herod's party presumably.

[2] A mountain fortress in Peræa on the boundary between Palestine and Arabia.

This statement of Flavius Josephus is sufficiently categorical. It states clearly that John the Baptizer was a very remarkable prophetical reformer of the day and that his following was very considerable. John's 'sayings,' Josephus tells us, had an astonishingly persuasive power over the Jewish populace. Herod fears John's influence and is convinced that he could do anything he pleases with the people. But what interests us most in this unfortunately too short statement is the reference to the nature of John's practice and teaching. His proclamation to the Jews, like that of all the prophets before him, was a strenuous call to righteousness,—they were to practise righteous dealings with one another (love of neighbour) and piety to God (love of God). There was also an external rite of baptism; but it had to be preceded by a cleansing of the soul through the fulfilling of this duty to neighbour and to God. Josephus particularly points out that the public washing or dipping was by no means intended as a magical rite, which so many believed in those days capable of washing away sins. The baptism was not a daily practice, Josephus seems to imply, as among the Essenes and other sects, but a public corporate act; and therefore the historian is clearly in error in regarding it as simply for the purifying of the body. On the contrary, it distinctly conveys the impression of being designed as an outer testimony to some belief—an act of faith.

The N.T. Account: The Dress and Food of Repentance.

And now let us pass to our New Testament information. Without laying stress on the details of the story of John's infancy as given in the third gospel, reminiscent as they may be of the Old Testament birth-stories of the old-time national heroes Isaac, Samson and Samuel, not to mention the coincidence that the two heroines of the gospel birth-narratives bear the names of Miriam and Elisheba, the sister and wife respectively of Aaron, the first priest, we may very reasonably believe, as it is stated, that John was of priestly descent; and therefore in every probability he was well versed, if not highly trained, in the scriptures.

Vowed from his birth to God by his parents, his strange dress and peculiar ascetic mode of life are quite in keeping with prophetical traditions, and thus of the schools of the prophets and of the Nazirs. As the prophets of old, notably Elijah, he wore a skin robe. But in keeping with the spiritual significance of his whole teaching, which will be more fully brought out in the sequel, such an outer sign in high probability had an inner meaning for this great proclaimer of repentance, of the turning back of Israel in contrition unto God.

Now there were certain Palestinian pre-Christian allegorists or exponents of the scriptures on quasi-mystical lines called Dorshē Reshumōth. According to a Rabbinic legend, going back along this line of interpretation, the ancient myth of Gen. 3₂₁ was conceived more spiritually. After the fall, the first falling away from God, Yahveh-Elohīm clothed Adam and Eve in coats of skin ('ōr), not because of their nakedness, but in exchange for their lost paradisaical garments of light ('ōr).

John lived at a time when such mystical interpretations, with a host of prophetical and apocalyptic notions, were in the air. It might very well then be that he himself in wearing a skin-robe intended something more than a simple copying of the fashion of the ancient prophets. In keeping with his ruling idea he may have thought it a most appropriate outer sign of repentance, a return to the first garments of fallen man, the proper robe of penitent sinners, and therefore especially of a leader who would show the people a whole-hearted example of turning again to God, thus retracing in a contrary direction the way of the fall.

So too with regard to food, there must be a return to the primitive law laid down for primal fallen man (Gen. 1_29): "Behold, I have given you every herb bearing seed, which is upon the face of the earth, and every tree, in which is the fruit of a tree yielding seed; to you it shall be for meat." It was only after the Deluge that men were permitted to eat animal food, according to the Noahic covenant as it is called. Imbued with ideas of penitence and repentance, John would desire to return to the strictest food-regulations of the earliest days of the fall, in keeping with his symbolic manner of clothing. Not only so, but seemingly with a refinement of self-discipline as a means of contrition, John chose from out the many 'fruits from a tree yielding seed' that of the carob or locust-tree, which was considered by the Jewish allegorists the most appropriate food of repentance. For we have preserved from this line of tradition an ancient proverb: "Israel needs carob-pods to make him repent," said to be based on a prophecy in Isaiah (1_20,) which the Midrash (*Wayikra Rabba*, 35) quotes as: "If ye be willing and obedient, the good of the land shall ye eat; but if ye refuse and resist, carob-pods shall ye eat"—where the last clause differs considerably from the R.V., which reads: "ye shall be devoured by the sword." Perhaps the 'husks' eaten by the Prodigal in the gospel-parable may in the original Aramaic have been carob-pods (Lk. 15:16). Much controversy has raged round the 'locusts' eaten by John, and early versions are various.

As for drink,—in addition to water for general purposes, John is said to have in particular sipped the honey of the wild bees. Why is this brought into so great prominence? Again perhaps this custom was determined for John by the same circle of ideas. He probably bethought him of Deut. 32:13: "He made him to suck honey out of the rock," and also of Ps. 81:16: "And with honey out of the rock shall I satisfy thee." From such considerations it may plausibly be believed that John adopted an asceticism of repentance with regard to clothing and food as completely in accordance with the scriptures as possible, and this in addition to the customary discipline of a vowed Nazir, 'consecrated' or 'made holy' as such from birth. The technical term for a Nazir is a Nazirite unto God, or holy unto God, as of Samson (LXX. Judges, 13:7, 16:9),—in brief God's 'holy one.'

Popular Messianic Expectations.

According to Josephus the great fear of Herod was that the reformatory movement of John would develop into a dangerous political Messianic revolt. The populace was on the tip-toe of expectation; many rumours were afloat as to the nature of the long-expected God's Anointed. Some thought he was to be a Nazir who would free Israel from their present foes, even as in days of old the Nazir Samson had freed them from the yoke of the Philistines. Moreover the well-known prophecy (Is. 11:1) about the 'sprout' from the root or stem of Jesse gave rise to much speculation, helped out by that word-play which exercised so powerful a fascination over the imaginative minds of the Jews of that day, and long before and after over other minds in many other lands. Now 'sprout' in Hebrew is *neṣer* or *nezer*; and this *neṣer* was to be the longed-for 'saviour' (again *neṣer*)—sounding so well together with *nazir*. Indeed, as was thought, he must needs be a Nazarai-an (Heb. *noṣeri*, Gk. *nazōrai-os*). Or again, as others expected, he was to be a carpenter (Aram. *bar nasar*), this being, according to a Samaritan Midrash, as we shall see in the sequel, in association with the expectation that the coming Redeemer was to be a second Noah, spiritually hewing and preparing the timber for a new ark of salvation.

All this was in the air and widespread; it is then quite believable, whether John himself made any such claims or no, that there were many rumours current of a Messianic purport concerning the strange appearance and powerful appeal of the renowned Baptizer. His Nazarite vow, his garb and diet of repentance, his confident proclamation of the very near approach of the catastrophic end of this æon or age or world,—all would conspire to make some, if not many, think that he himself was the great Nazir-Neṣer, the expected 'holy one' of God. By others he was thought to be Elijah returned, as the prophet Malachi (the Book of the Angel or Messenger of Yahveh) had foretold (4₅): "Behold, I will send you Elijah the prophet before the great and terrible Day of the Lord come"; or even, may be, some thought that that prophet of promise like unto Moses (Deut. 18₁₅) had been raised up in John. John himself apparently made no claim to be any of these; he was a proclaimer of the near approach of the great and terrible Day and a powerful exhorter to repentance. It is doubtful even whether he gave himself out to be simply "the voice of one crying in the wilderness" (Mk. 1₃); for such a knower of the scriptures would have been aware that the original of Isaiah 40₃ read: "The voice of one crying: In the wilderness, etc." But apparently John was not only an inspired prophet, he was also a wonder-worker, if certain echoes concerning him in the Synoptics ring true. For there we read that because of his healing wonders Jesus was thought by some to be John returned from the dead, and that the same accusation in this connection of being possessed by a demon brought against Jesus had also been brought against John.

The Sanctification of the Jordan-Water.

However all this may be, John was utterly convinced, not only that the time of the End was close at hand, but also that the prophecies were beginning to be fulfilled. But what of his characteristic baptizing in the Jordan of all places? This is taken as a simple historic fact which requires no explanation by the vast majority; but it presents a serious problem for those who are aware that in those days the brackish waters of the sluggish Jordan were deemed by theologians and ritualists as unfit for purificatory purposes. What then could have induced John to reject this priestly and purist tabū? The only feasible motive is to be found in supposing that John was convinced that a remarkable prophetical vision of Ezekiel (47₁₋₉), where the prophet is addressed as Son of Man, was being fulfilled. In the longed-for time of the Messianic deliverance a mighty stream of holy water from the temple-hill of Zion was to flow down and heal the waters of the unclean Jordan-land, the Arabah or Desert.

Eisler has acutely conjectured that this idea of a fount of living and healing water for Israel goes back ultimately to Isaiah 28$_{16}$, not however as it stands at present in the R.V. wording, but in its extended form which was well known up to the 3rd century A.D. This reads as follows according to his rendering: "Behold, I lay down in Zion a living stone, a stone of probation, a precious threshold-stone for a foundation. Out of its hollow shall flow forth rivers of living water; he that believeth on me shall not suffer from drought."

This was naturally taken by the allegorists of the time in a spiritual sense, even as they explained the water miraculously supplied to the Israelites in the Desert as a figure for the Torah or Law. The living water signified the Word of Yahveh, the outpouring of the spirit of God. Thus the Messianic Spring of living water could well be believed to typify an intensification or consummation of the Divine Law, heralding the manifestation of the Sovereignty of God in the Last Days. But spiritual reality and material happenings were never widely divorced in the mind of a pious Jew, and thus there was a literal meaning as well to be given to prophecy.

The Probable Symbolic Significance of John's Baptism.

If all this is well conceived, it is not difficult to understand what Josephus tells us of John's method, though the proper sense of John's motive seems to have escaped the historian. Deeply stirred by the strenuous exhortations of the teacher and the extraordinary power of a proclaimer so utterly convinced of the near coming of the terrible Day, little wonder that the people, just as in evangelical revivals of our own day, were filled with an agony of penitence which would find relief only in a public confession of their sins. Thereafter they were plunged in the Jordan, signifying no external washing, but a very drowning as it were of the old body of sin in that now sacred stream to which faith ascribed life-redeeming properties, a regeneration wrought by the saving spring of God's outpouring flowing down from the sanctuary into the desert. If they repented, if they once unfeignedly turned again to God, then would the prophetical promise in Micah 7$_{19}$ be fulfilled: "He will turn again, he will have compassion upon us, he will subdue our iniquities. Yea, thou wilt wash away all our sins into the depths of the sea."

The Baptism of the Proselytes.

But in practising this baptismal rite John was running counter to far more than the priestly purist tabū which regarded the Jordan water as unfit for purification. He was baptizing *Israelites*, and in so doing putting the Chosen ones on a level with those gentiles who had to submit to a bath of purification before they could be admitted to the privileges of the sons of Abraham. A proselyte or a 'new-comer' (*advena*) who would join the church or ecclesia of Israel, had to submit to a baptismal rite, the pre-Christian origin of which is no longer disputed. It was a bath not only of purification but also of regeneration in the presence of legal witnesses. The candidate stood in the water and listened to a short discourse consisting of commandments from the Law. Thereon the gentile convert dipped completely under the water, signifying the drowning of his previous impious and idolatrous self. Thereafter he arose reborn a true Israelite. And this new birth was taken in a very literal sense, for after the rite the neophyte, or 'new-born babe,' could no longer inherit from his former gentile relatives; not only so, but according to Rabbinic casuistry he could not even commit incest with one of them. This regenerative gentile baptism (*tebilah gerīm*) was made by the theologians to depend from the promise in Ezekiel (36:25-26): "I will sprinkle clean water upon you, and ye shall be clean: from all your filthiness and from all your idols, will I cleanse you. A new heart I will give you, and a new spirit will I put within you."

But this prophecy clearly applied to Israel only. It could never have been intended as the sanction of a customary rite for converted gentiles. It is thus very credible that a fervent eschatologist, filled with Messianic expectations, such as John, would conceive the promise as foreshadowing a unique miraculous event of the Last Days. Moreover John's insistence on baptism for the Jews, at a time when their religious leaders thought it necessary to impose baptism on gentile converts as a purificatory regenerative rite making them fit to be associated religiously with the naturally born sons of Abraham, seems clearly to have been dictated by the deeper spiritual conviction that it was Israel itself who required regeneration. For John, from the standpoint of spiritual values, the Jews were no more a privileged people; they had forfeited their birthright; Israel itself was now no better than the heathen. Physical kinship with Abraham could no longer be considered a guarantee against the Wrath to come. To escape the trials and terrors of that Day the only way for them was to repent, and so become members of the new spiritual Israel by submitting to a rite similar to that which they arrogantly imposed on the gentiles. What greater humiliation than this could there be to the racial pride of the Jew? But things were so desperate, that it required even this act of humiliation as an earnest of truly sincere repentance and contrition. Unrepentant they were no better than heathen idolaters.

ONE OF JOHN'S DISCOURSES AND ITS SYMBOLISM.

Let us now turn to the first part of the short but powerful address of the Baptizer handed on by Mt. (3_{7-10}) and Lk. (3_{7-9}), a most interesting example of those stirring utterances or 'sayings' of his referred to by Josephus.

> Ye out-births of vipers, who hath given you a glimpse of fleeing from the Wrath to come? Make fruit, therefore, worthy of (or sufficient for) your repentance. And think not (Lk. begin not) to say within (or among) yourselves: We have Abraham [for] father. For I say unto you that God is able of these stones (Aram. *'ab'nayya*) to raise (or wake) up children (Aram. *b'nayya*) for Abraham. But even now the axe is laid unto the root of the trees: every tree, therefore, which beareth not good fruit, is hewn down and cast into the fire.

This graphic discourse, contained in Q, begins with the same terrible phrase 'generation' or 'out-births of vipers' which Jesus also uses on several occasions. It may possibly go back to Micah 7_{17}, where we read, referring to the heathen: "They shall lick the dust like serpents, like those creeping on the earth." And if 'licking the dust' can be taken in the sense of the allegorists of the time, who interpret it as eating excrement, a fate allotted to the serpent-shaped souls of the damned in Sheōl, it becomes all the more strikingly graphic. In vain do they think they will escape because they are of kinship with Abraham, or that God cannot repeat the wonder he once wrought, of raising up children out of the barren rock of their forefather. God is able to make a new Israel out of the very stones, just as he had of old hewn, like stones (Heb. *'abanīm*), a line of sons (Heb. *bānīm*) from the once barren rock of Abraham, as Isaiah says (51₁₋₂): "Look unto the rock whence ye were hewn . . . look unto Abraham your father."

This for the 'stones'; but what of the 'trees'? There are other passages in the O.T. (*e.g.* Ps. 1₁, Jer. 17₅₋₈) which liken the man who delights in the Law and has faith in Yahveh to fruit-bearing trees; but the most arresting verse in this connection is to be found in the continuation of the same vision in Ezekiel (47₁₋₈) which so graphically depicted the Messianic Source. This reads (v. 12):

"By the river upon the banks thereof, on this side and on that side, shall grow all trees for meat, whose leaf shall not fade; they shall bring forth new fruit month after month, because their waters issue from the sanctuary: and the fruit thereof shall be for meat and the leaf thereof for medicine."

The mystical application of this prophetical utterance to the righteous of Israel as the fruit-bearing trees of the longed-for days of the Messiah, would surely strike the imagination of so intuitive a mind as John's; it is indeed all of a piece with his general conception and expectation and fits in most deftly.

The Fish and Fishers Symbolism.

But this does not exhaust the imagery of Ezekiel's striking vision of the outpouring of God's spirit in the days of the End, which made so deep an impression upon John. The prophet uses another graphic figure, which also greatly influenced early Christianity and was made much of later on in the symbolic interpretations of some of the Church Fathers. If only we had the mystical exegesis of this figure as conceived in the mind of the pre-Christian Palestinian Dorshē Rashumōth, who anticipated in some ways the Alexandrian Jewish allegorists of Philo's day, we should probably find that they had already given spiritual significance to the following arresting verses (9 and 10) of the vision. These read in Eisler's rendering:

"Wheresoever the river shall come, everything that moveth shall live; and there shall be a very great multitude of fish, because the waters shall come thither. . . . And it shall come to pass [that] the fishers stand by it from En-Gedi unto En-Eglaim; they shall be [a place] to spread forth nets [for all fish] according to their kinds."

En-Gedi and En-Eglaim were two oases with freshwater springs—the Gedi or Kid Spring and the Eglaim or (?) Calf Spring—on the shores of the Dead Sea or Salt Lake. The former was the chief centre of the Essenes. With such a striking figure before him it would be easy for John, the proclaimer of repentance and the turning again to God of a righteous remnant, to believe that in the Days of the End there were to be prophets who should be 'fishers of men.'

Now it is remarkable that we have a number of references to this fishing of souls bound up with echoes of legends of John the Baptizer, which blend into a rich stream of Gnostic traditions which still exists to-day and goes back eventually to very early times.

The Mandæans, that is believers in the Mandā or Gnosis, or Nazorāyā as they call themselves, known to the Arabs as the Sūbbā's or Baptists, have much to tell us of the 'Fisher of Souls' and the evil 'fishers of men,' as we shall see later on.

Their saga of the Fisher of Souls is a beautiful conception within the setting of eschatological and soteriological notions, and seems to be an integral element of the syncretic stream of the Mandā which goes back far towards Gnostic beginnings. Now the Mandæan traditions are hostile not only to Christianity but also to Judaism. Many of their notions can be closely paralleled with some of the doctrines of the religion of Mānī, with some of the main elements underlying the scheme of the Coptic Gnostic Pistis Sophia and the two treatises of the Bruce Codex; points of contact may also be found in what we know of the doctrines of the Elchasaites, and in some parts of the Clementine romances which preserve early Ebionite traditions and legends of Simon the Magian, with whom John is brought into connection.

And here it may be noted that, if it is surprising to find the influence of John the Baptizer spreading as far east as Mesopotamia, it is not out of keeping with the fact that the baptism of John was also practised in the east Mediterranean area far outside Palestine among the Dispersion and indeed among some of the early Christian communities, as we learn from the Acts and Epistles, witness especially the Apollōs incident (Acts 18:24, I. Cor. 1:12).

Ḥani-Ōannēs-Iōannēs.

No little of mythic notions from old Babylonian, Chaldæan and Iranian traditions is to be found immixed in the oldest deposits of this Mandæan stream; there is thus a pre-Christian background as well. Indeed the Fisher-figure cannot fail at once to remind students of the comparative science of religion of the ancient Babylonian fish-clad fisher-god Ḥani-Ōannēs—the archaic Ea, father of Marduk the saviour-god of Babylon who rose yearly from the dead. This primeval God of Wisdom was the culture-god who had taught early mankind all the arts of civilization. Berossus, the Chaldæan priest who wrote for the Greeks a history of his people, tells us of no less than six manifestations of Ōannēs in successive periods; and this notion of revelation and saving in successive periods is fundamental with the Mandæans. Ōannēs rose from the sea—the waters presumably of the Persian Gulf, in the old story; but Marduk, his son, descended from heaven.

It is by no means improbable that the picturing of appropriate ancient myths which floated freely in the thought-atmosphere of Babylonia, may have determined some of the imagery of Ezekiel's visions by the 'river of Babylon,' and indeed may otherwise have psychically influenced indirectly no little of Jewish apocalytic literature, as for instance when the Ezra Apocalypse (at the end of the 1st century A.D.) tells us that the Redeemer of the world, the Celestial Man, is expected to rise from the 'heart of the ocean.' If then, as Ezra IV. permits us to conclude, certain apocalyptists and allegorists, who were probably Jews of the Babylonian or Syrian Dispersion, could conceive of their pre-existent Messiah as in some way associated with the figure of the ancient Ḥani (Ōannēs, Iannēs, Iōannes), and expected the Redeemer of Israel to arise from the depths of the great waters, it is not improbable that in those days, when the interplay of mystical associations was so prevalent and eagerly sought out, some of the most enthusiastic followers of John may have believed that this baptizing 'fisher of souls' was the expected manifestation.

JOHN-JONAH.

Similarity in the sounds of names fascinated men's minds, and Ḥani-Ōannēs-John is not the only name-play we meet with in the Baptist's story. Attempts have been made by scholars to show that 'the sign of the prophet Jonah' (Q—Matth. 12$_{19f.}$=Lk. 11$_{29f.}$) was perhaps originally connected with John, and that a testimony of Jesus to John has been converted already in Q, the early non-Markan source of matter common to Mt. and Lk., into a testimony of Jesus concerning himself. (On this point see Eisler, *op. cit.*, pp. 156-162, where all is set out in detail.) It is further of interest to note that Jonah in Hebrew means Dove, and that among the Mandæans there was a class of the perfect called Doves. Compare also the Greek *Physiologus* (xli.): "The Dove . . . which is John the Baptist." The names Jonah and John could easily be brought into close connection, and indeed Jonah is sometimes found as a shortened form of Joḥanan.

The Jonah-legend provided a very suitable setting wherein to depict the life of a prophet who caused his hearers to repent, and it may be that Jesus referred to John as 'a greater Jonah' (Mt. 12$_{41}$.). The most striking image in the mythic story is the Great Fish. Now the belly of the Great Fish for the Jewish allegorists, and indeed it is plainly stated in the legend itself, was Sheōl, the Underworld, the Pit. But another mythic Great

Fish, or perhaps the same in another aspect, was the cosmic monster Leviāthān. And symbolists, allegorists and mystics got busy with this mythic figure. Thus we find that Leviāthān was the name given by the Ophites of Celsus, who are plainly of Syrian Babylonian origin, to the Seven,—that is to the cosmic animal psychē, the hierarchy of rulers and devourers of the animal souls of men as well as of animals proper, each of the Seven being symbolized by an animal figure, probably an animal-faced (lion, etc.) dragon or fish. In the Mandæan tradition the Fisher of Souls takes the Seven in his net and destroys them, even as in the old Babylonian myth the Saviour-god Manduk catches Tiamāt, their mother, the primeval dragon of the deep, in his net and destroys her. And strangely enough there is an old Rabbinical legend of Jonah preserved in the *Midrash Yalqut Yona* (§1), which relates that, when the prophet was in the belly of the Great Fish, he prayed that it should carry him quickly to the Leviāthān, so that he might catch it with his fishing tackle. For Jonah desired, when once again safely ashore, to make of its flesh a feast for the righteous, —a distinct reference to the Messianic fish-banquet which is to take place in the days of the End.

The Jewish folk of the Babylonian dispersion, who were surrounded with images of the fish-clad Ḥani-Ōannēs and of his priests, would easily think of them as representing a man swallowed by a fish, and as easily be reminded of the story of their great prophet Jonah, who was fabled to have made the proud King of Ashshur and all the Ninevites repent; and the mystics subsequently would easily associate all this with Messianic notions.

Rabbinic Fish-symbolism.

It has recently been shewn by that acute scholar J. Scheftelowitz from hitherto neglected Rabbinical documents that 'fish' was quite a common symbol for the righteous man of Israel, who lived all his life in the waters of the Torah or Sacred Law. The evidence goes back as early as the times of Rabban Gamaliel the Elder, the teacher of Paul, who was therefore a contemporary of John and Jesus. Thus we read in the *Midrash Tanḥuma* to Deut. 5$_{32}$: "As a fish delights in water, even so a master of the scriptures dives into the streams of balm"—the sweet smelling waters of the Law; compare the sweet savour and perfume of the gnōsis and of the heavenly essences and *per contra* the stench of the evil fishers or teachers of false doctrine in the Mandæan John-Book. Decisive in this connection is the following passage from the *Aboth de R. Nathan* (ch. 40):

"The pupils of Rabbi Gamaliel the Elder were divided into four kinds of fish: into clean and unclean [brackish water] fish from the Jordan and fish from the Ocean, according to their high and low descent and to the degree of their learning and quickness of their understanding."

Though they were not 'fishers of men,' they were fish of Yahveh swimming in the holy stream, the life-giving waters of the Law. It was thus very natural for John, remembering the striking passage in Ezekiel (47$_{12}$) about the fish who repented, to contrast with them the unrepentant as a 'generation of vipers,' (cp. the fish-scorpion contrast in Mt. 7$_{10}$). Nor could John have been ignorant of the prophecy in Jeremiah

(16₁₆) concerning the gathering together of dispersed Israel: "Behold, I will send for many fishers, saith the Lord, and they shall fish them," and have given it a spiritual significance. But of an even more arresting nature is the following from *Berešith Rabba* (ch. 97):

"As the Israelites are innumerable, even so are the fishes; as the Israelites will never die out on the earth, the fishes will never die out in their element. Only the Son of Man named 'Fish' could lead Israel into the Land of Promise,—namely Joshuah ben Nun (= Fish)." The Greek transliteration of Joshuah in the LXX. version is invariably Jesus.

The Samaritan Ta'eb—a Reborn Joshuah or Noah.

Now in Samaritan tradition, and it will be remembered that the Samaritans rejected all the Jewish scriptures save the Five Fifths of the Law, their future Redeemer was to be called Joshuah. This Deliverer they called the Ta'eb, the Returner, and they believed he would be a reborn or returned Joshuah. The Ta'eb is the Samaritan 'Messiah.' In this connection a recently translated Samaritan Midrash (B.M. Samaritan MS. Or. 3393[1]) is especially instructive. It understands the title Ta'eb as signifying 'he who repents' or even 'he who makes to repent,' not so much the Returner as the Turner-back of others. It is brought into close connection also with Noham, meaning Repenting, and is thus by word-play associated with Noah. Our Samaritan Midrash accordingly brings Noah on to the scene of expected redemption, and becomes a spiritualized version of the Deluge-story, abounding in mystical word-plays. One or two speci-

---

[1] Ed. by Adalbert Merx, *Zeitschr. f. alt. Wiss.*, 1909, xvii. 80.

mens of them may now be given, as the ideas behind them are reminiscent of the John-circle of ideas.

Whereas in the old story Yahveh orders Noah: "Make thee an ark (t^ebah)," the Midrash makes God say unto the Ta'eb: "Make thee a conversion"—or repentance (Aram. *shuba, tubah*). And so it continues in many details glossing the original parts of the ark by means of word-play, introducing notions of propitiation, expiation and atonement. A single passage from the original will make this clear, and in reading it we should remember that Samaria was a hot-bed of mystic and gnostic movements of all sorts.

Behold I bring a [flood of] conversion [and] of divine favour upon the earth, to save Israel and gather it from everywhere under the sky. I shall perform my covenant, which I have set up with Abraham, Isaac and Jacob. And thou shalt enter into the conversion, thou and thy house and the whole house of Israel with thee; and take with thee all kind of . . . praying and fasting and purification, which thou performest, and take all unto thee, and it shall be for conversion for thee and for them. And the Ta'eb did everything as God had commanded him.

The ark (t^ebah) saved Noah from the flood of perdition, and the conversion (*shubah, tubah*) will save the Penitent One (*Ta'eb*) and all the sons of Israel from the [flood of] perversion.

The 'flood of perversion' is that of 'the cursed æon.' Among the many Messianic expectations of those days, therefore, was the belief that in the Last Days it would again be as in the times of Noah, as indeed we are expressly informed by Q (Mt. $24_{37ff.}$ = Lk. $17_{26ff.}$).

John's Eschatological Symbolism.

There are other points of interest in the fragmentary 'sayings' of John and other references preserved in the synoptic accounts, but of these we shall select only one as being of special interest. John's expectation of the nature of the catastrophe of the times of the End was somewhat complex. Three phases of elemental destruction haunted his imagination. Similar disasters had already happened in the past at the culmination of certain successive critical periods in the history of mankind. There had been a destruction by water, another by a mighty wind and tempest which overwhelmed the great Tower (to which many a Rabbinic legend testifies), and a destruction by fire in the days of Lot. John's baptism or water-purification may well have been intended as an outer sign of the inner attempt to avert from the righteous the dire results of the great forthcoming world 'trial' by the water of God's Wrath that would overwhelm the wicked. But there were two other 'baptisms' or purifications which he expected a greater than himself to effect in similar fashion and for a similar purpose. There was to be a purification or baptism by fire; and, in Christian interpretation, the third and last and greatest was to be effected by means of the holy 'spirit.' This would not be out of keeping with the belief of John, for it was ever the spirit of God, as water, fire or wind, that would purify and save the righteous. But the graphic figure of the winnowing fan in John's declaration shows clearly that the notion was connected in his mind with the necessary wind without which winnowing was impossible—the mighty wind or spirit of God. For the good this would result in a blessed harvesting, but for the evil it would be a scattering as of chaff.

Though all these notions may well have come to John within the ambit of the Jewish scriptures, many prophetical pronouncements in which graphically depict all these forms of Divine visitation, it is nevertheless not without significance that the rites of purification by water, fire and wind (ventilation) were an integral element of some of the Hellenistic mystery-institutions, and that the periodic catastrophic scheme is clearly to be paralleled in the later Babylonian astral religion, and especially in its blending with Iranian conceptions which centre round the æon-cult (Zervanism), and all those notions of the Great Year and world-periods, which later Stoicism took over and made familiar to Imperial times. This Great Year had three 'seasons' —summer, winter, spring—each of which was assigned to one of the three most ancient elements: fire, water and wind. As the Great Year turned on itself the constellations returned at the end of the revolution to the same positions they had occupied in a former Great Year. There were thus critical moments in the æonic movement, and at these cosmic catastrophes occurred.

It is hardly to be supposed that John had any such 'scientific' notions in his mind: but it is undeniable that many had such conceptions in his day, and indeed among the learned and mystics we find blends of such 'science' with prophetical intuitions. But for the Jewish eschatologist it was a once for all event he expected, whereas for such men as the Stoic thinkers it was a perpetual recurrence.

John and Jesus generally.

And what is the outcome of this enquiry? It seems to me that a very important background of Christian origins is here indicated. It points to a widespread Jewish eschatological and therefore necessarily Messianic movement prior to Christianity, of which earliest Christianity was at first a culmination, whatever modifications and completions were subsequently introduced. It is therefore to be regretted that our information concerning John the Baptizer and his doctrines is so meagre.

It is quite natural that some of John's adherents should have attached themselves to Jesus on his public appearance as a proclaimer before the martyrdom of their own imprisoned prophet. The suddenness with which Mk., our earliest narrative, introduces Jesus 'calling' the first four of his disciples and their instant leaving all and following him to become 'fishers of men,' is inexplicable without there having been some prior knowledge of the Way on the part of Simon and Andrew, James and John. They may well have already been familiar with John's teaching. Indeed the writer of the Fourth Gospel tells us categorically (Jn. 1:40) that Andrew, the brother of Simon-Peter-Kephas, had been a disciple of the Baptizer.

But if some of John's actual 'disciples' followed Jesus before any question of Messiahship arose, it is probable that far more of his lay-adherents also did so. Indeed the earliest history of the expansion of Christianity, that is of the Jesus Messianic movement, preserves traces that in some places there was a considerable Johannine influence, notably the continued use of John's baptism. On the contrary, most of John's disciples to all seeming refused to recognize the Jesus Messianic claims, and the echoes of history preserved in the Mandæan traditions declare that they most emphatically rejected them.

In any case it may well be that some of the great figures, types and symbols used by Jesus in his exhortations and teaching were not original to him, but that he shared them, together with other mystic, apocalyptic and prophetical notions, with circles that had been instructed by John. Jesus is made to distinguish John as the greatest prophet who had come before him, nay as more than a prophet; and yet the least in the Kingdom of Heaven is said to be greater than a John. This can only mean in the Kingdom in its fulness; for surely most of the Christians fell far short of the high virtue of the Baptist. What is furthermore exceedingly probable, if not unquestionably evident, is that the whole of John's mentality was flooded with what we can only call mystic notions and conceits, graphic figures, highly spiritualized, the mentality of a prophet and seer. If John is the forerunner of Jesus, many of the Baptizer's eschatological and associated beliefs are probably the forerunners of earliest Christian general doctrine. And with all this in mind, it is difficult not to believe that Jesus not only knew more of John personally and what lay at the back of him, but used more of his ideas and symbolisms than the gospels would lead us to suppose.

The Mandæan tradition deserves most careful analysis from this point of view; but before presenting it we may add a few words on the estrangement of the John- and Jesus-movements.

John and the Messiahship of Jesus.

Though the Synoptics in some passages are at pains to let it appear as if John recognized the Messiahship of Jesus, and the later and 'correcting' Fourth Gospel emphatically affirms that he did so from the baptism onwards, there was evidently very considerable doubt on the question in the earliest tradition. Q (Matth. 11$_{3f.}$ = Lk. 7$_{19f.}$) lets the reader see that John to the end had no conviction, much less prior spiritual apperception, on the subject. For it tells us that just before his end the imprisoned prophet sent messengers to Jesus asking him in complete uncertainty: "Art thou he that should come, or look we for another?" To this unambiguous question no direct answer is given. John's disciple-messengers are bidden simply to report to their master the wonderful healings of which they have been told or which they have witnessed. The proof of Messiahship is made here to rest solely on wonder-doings; any prior spiritual recognition by John of Jesus as the Expected One is unknown to this tradition, nor is it able to report that John accepted the wonders as proof of the fulfilment of his expectation. From this we may reasonably feel assured that, though some of John's disciples followed Jesus when he began his public ministry after John had been put in prison, and continued the proclamation of the near Coming of the Kingdom, the majority refrained. They continued in their own way and discipline; nor did they subsequently recognize the Messiahship of Jesus, for above all they had no authority from their master to do so.

This is a negative inference; but the positive rejection of the Christian Messianic claim is brought out with sharp polemical emphasis in the Mandæan tradition, which claims to derive from John and regards Jesus as the Deceiver-Messiah. The baptism of Jesus by John is acknowledged, but explained in polemic mystic fashion. There are however signs that, apart from the subsequent bitterness of outer theological controversy, there was originally an inner deeper gnostic-ground of division, for Jesus is not represented as unknowing, but on the contrary, is made to answer certain test questions of John with profound moral insight. But the most surprising fact of Mandæan tradition is that it preserves no indications of having entertained any belief in distinctive Jewish Messianism at all. Its soteriology is peculiar to itself and the tradition repudiates Jewish prophecy and apocalyptic and in fact the whole Torah, as emphatically as it does Christian doctrine. Nevertheless on its own showing, in the beginning the particular community of which John was so great a prophet, is depicted as settled in Judæa, even in Jerusalem, and is claimed to have had a profound knowledge of the inner meaning of the Law. It is made to look back to a still more ancient tradition which is claimed to be purer and wiser than that of the Hebrews. Though the legendary 'historical' side of the question is exceedingly obscure, our best authorities are agreed that, as far as the mythic element is concerned, the Mandæan tradition preserves many traces of the earliest forms of the pre-Christian Gnosis known to us. The problem is thus exceedingly complex.

II.

FROM THE JOHN-BOOK OF THE MANDÆANS.

WE will now proceed to see what the Gnostic John-folk have to say about the person of Yōhānā and concerning their early Palestinian community, and will conclude with some typical extracts from their John-Book collection, of which the most characteristic and important will be what may be called the sagas of the Fisher of Souls and of the Good Shepherd; but first a word or two as to our sources of information.

INTRODUCTORY.

The Mandæans (lit. Gnostics—*mandā = gnōsis*) of the lower Euphrates are the only known surviving community of the ancient Gnosis. That they have survived to our own day[1] is a remarkable testimony to the strength of their convictions and of loyalty to a tradition which they claim to go back to pre-Christian days. The documents call them Nāzōræans.[2] The Arabs generally refer to them as Sūbbā's or Baptists, while the first Portuguese Jesuit missionaries of the Inquisi-

[1] In 1875 N. Siouffi, the French Vice-Consul at Mosul, estimated them at some 4,000 souls in all (*Etudes sur la Religion des Soubbas ou Sabéens*, Paris, 1880). These were then to be found chiefly in the neighbourhood of Basra and Kūt. Siouffi's estimate, however, was certainly too low; for Shaikh K. Dojaily, Lecturer in Arabic at the School of Oriental Studies, informs me that he quite recently obtained from the supreme head of all the communities at Naziriyah the precise statistics, and that they still number about 10,000 men, women and children.

[2] This is a very ancient general designation used by a number of early sects. It has nothing to do with Nazareth (Q. Nazara), which is quite unknown outside the gospel-narratives, not to speak of the philological impossibility of such a word-formation as Nazoræan from Nazareth. Lidzbarski rejects W. B. Smith's (in *Der vorchristliche Jesus*, Giessen, 1906) derivation—Nazar-Ya (= Jehoshua—Jesus — Sotēr—Saviour), and makes out a good case for origin in $\sqrt{\text{NZR}}$, with the meaning of 'to observe'; hence 'Observers'—sc. of the laws or ordinances or may be of the holy life (*Liturgies*, pp. xvi.ff.).

tion erroneously introduced them to Europe in the early part of the 17th century as the 'Christians of St. John.' But Christians they certainly are not; on the contrary they have ever been strenuously opposed to Christianity, though they may have sometimes so camouflaged themselves to avoid Moslim persecution in the first place and the Inquisitional methods of the missionaries in the second.

The Mandæan religious literature (for of secular literature there is none) supplies us with the richest direct sources of any phase of ancient Gnosticism which we possess; these documents are also all the more valuable because they are purely Oriental without any Hellenistic immixture. Indeed our only other considerable direct sources, that is sources not contaminated or rendered suspect by transmission through hostile hands, are the Trismegistic literature, the Coptic Gnostic documents and the recent Manichæan finds in Tūrfān. The Mandæan language is little used by the faithful except for religious purposes. The M. communities in general have for long used Arabic as their common speech, though one or more groups speak Persian. Mandæan is a South Babylonian dialect of Aramæan, its nearest cognate being the Northern Babylonian as in the Babylonian Talmūd. Their graceful script is peculiar to the Mandæans; the vowels are in full lettering and are not indicated by points or other diacritical marks.

Their literature was once far more extensive; for what we possess is manifestly in the form of extracts collected from manifold more ancient sources, which are no longer extant.

The chief existing documents are as follows:

1. The *Sidrā Rabbā* (Great Book) or *Genzā*

(Treasury), which is divided into Right and Left pages, for the living and the deceased respectively, it is said but I am told that in some copies the alternate pages are reversed and in some ceremonies read simultaneously by two readers facing each other. It consists of sixty-four pieces or tractates,—theological, cosmological, mythological, ethical and historical. This collection is indubitably prior to the Mohammedan conquest (*cir.* 651 A.D.), and its sources are of course far more ancient.

2. The *Sidrā d'Yahyā* (Book of John), also called *Drāshē d'Malkē* (Discourses of the [Celestial] Kings). A considerable number of its pieces, which can be listed under thirty-seven headings, deal with the life and teachings of John the Baptizer. Yahyā is the Arabic form of John, the Mandæan Yōhānā, Heb. Yoḥanan; the two forms, Arabic and Mandæan, alternate and show that the collection was made, or more probably redacted, after the Moslim conquest.

3. The *Qolastā* (Quintessence or Selection, called also the Book of Souls)—Liturgies for the Baptismal Ceremony, the Service for the Departed (called the 'Ascent'—*Masseqtā*) and for the Marriage Ritual. These hymns and prayers are lofty, though most of them are presumably not so ancient as those in the *Genzā*.

4. The *Dīvān*, containing the procedure for the expiation of certain ceremonial offences and sketches of the 'regions' through which the soul must pass in its ascent.

5. The *Asfar Malwāshē* (Book of the Zodiacal Constellations).

6. Certain inscriptions on earthen cups and also pre-Mohammedan lead tablets.

It would not be difficult to prepare an annotated bibliography (as we have done elsewhere for the Coptic Gnostic *Pistis Sophia* document) tracing the history of the development of Mandæan study in the West from the 17th century onwards, but this is a sketch not a treatise. It is sufficient to say that, owing to the difficulty of the language, no one did any work of permanent value on the texts till the Dutch scholar A. J. H. Wilhelm Brandt published his arresting studies —*Die Mandäische Religion* (Leipzig, 1884) and *Mandäische Schriften* (Göttingen, 1893), the latter containing a version of selected pieces from the *Genzā*. Brandt was the real pioneer translator (basing himself on Nöldeke's indispensable Mandæan Grammar, 1875); his predecessors were either entirely ignorant of the language or indulged mainly in guess-work. Brandt's art. 'Mandæans' in Hastings' *Encyclopædia of Religion and Ethics* (1915) is a valuable summary of his most matured views, and to it I would refer my readers as the best general Introduction available.[1] Brandt's philological equipment in so difficult and rare a dialect as Mandæan, however, was not sufficient for the work of full translation. Moreover he does not seem to me to have sufficiently realized the great importance of the subject for the general history of pre-Christian and early Christian Gnosticism. This, however, was fully recognized by the late Prof. Wilhelm Bousset, who devoted

---

[1] Brandt passed away from this scene of his labours on March 4, 1915, and his posthumous work *Die Mandäer: ihre Religion und ihre Geschichte* (Trans. of Koninklijke Akadamie van Wetenshappen te Amsterdam, Nov., 1915) is practically a German edition of this article. Kessler's art. 'Mandäer' (*Redencyk. f. prot. Theolog.*, 3rd ed., Herzog-Hauck, Leipzig, 1903) is a helpful study; it entirely supersedes his *Enc. Brit.*, 9th ed., art. K. avers that the M. literature preserves the oldest form of the Gnosis known to us. Art. 'Mandæans,' *Enc. Brit.*, 11th ed., 1911, is stated to be part K. and part G. W. Thatcher; it is a poor production even as a summary of K.'s later art. It is short, contemptuous and superficial, and deprives the reader of much that is most valuable in K. in the shape of references and parallels. It would have been really better to have translated K. literally.

many pages of his admirable study *Hauptprobleme der Gnosis* (Göttingen, 1907) to showing the enormous light which the earliest deposits of the *Genzā* throw on pre- and non-Christian Gnostic notions. Indeed in this work Bousset gave a quite new historical perspective to Gnostic studies, and showed the great importance of the Mandæan, Coptic Gnostic and Manichæan documents, when critically treated, for tracing the genesis and development of the widespread Gnosis of antiquity, which had its proximate origin in the influence of Persian ideas on Babylonian religious traditions from the time of the Great Kings (6th century B.C.) onwards, with further Hellenistic immixture and modifications after the conquest of Alexander the Great (last third of 4th century B.C.). There is also a parallel blending and Hellenization of Egyptian mystery-lore as seen most clearly in the Trismegistic tradition. More recently Prof. R. Reitzenstein, who has done such excellent work on the Trismegistic Gnosis and on the Hellenistic mystery-religions, has published a valuable contribution to M. research in his *Das Mandäische Buch des Herrn der Grösse* (Heildelberg, 1919). Both these scholars are free from that apologetic tendency to which so few Christian scholars can rise superior in dealing with the Gnosis. But the *savant* to whom we owe most is Prof. Mark Lidzbarski, whose extraordinary knowledge of Aramæan dialects and allied Semitic linguistics has at last placed in our hands reliable versions of two of the M. collections: *Das Johannesbuch der Mandäer* (Giessen, 1915) and *Mandäische Liturgien* (Berlin, 1920). L. has also made a translation of the *Genzā*, the publication of which is eagerly expected.[1]

[1] On May 15, 1923, Dr. R. Eisler informed me: " L. writes that his trans. of *Genzā* is finished; printing will begin soon and take about a year and a half." Unfortunately since then the difficulties of publication in Germany have so

Until this appears it is not possible to be reasonably sure of all one's ground and so get an all-round perspective of it. Meantime, as no really adequate translation of any pieces have so far appeared in English,[1] I think it will be of service to give a selection of renderings from the German of Lidzbarski's John-Book, so that readers of these pages may become acquainted with specimens of the material, and be in a better position in some measure to appreciate for themselves its nature, quality and importance; for it may eventually turn out to be one of the most valuable indications we possess for Background of Christian Origins research. These renderings will be as close to the German as possible, so that readers may have L.'s version practically before them, and the inevitable leakage of translation from translation be reduced to a minimum. Even so, I hope that what seems to me to be the beauty of the original, will not be entirely evaporated. The major part of the material of the Liturgies is indubitably in verse; but the John-Book as well, if not also mainly in verse, as a most competent Aramæan scholar assures me, is clearly in rhythmic prose (*Kunstprosa*) and highly poetical. L., however, has not broken up the lines as in the Liturgies.

---

increased, that the arrangements for printing have fallen through, and this most indispensable basic source of information for students of the Mandæan Gnosis is accordingly held up.

[1] To be precise, in book-form; for I have already published the following versions in *The Quest* in the last two years; they are but a third of the translations I have made in MS. from the John-Book and the Liturgies. I say this, however, in no disparagement of Miss A. L. B. Hardcastle's sympathetic and painstaking studies, containing some versions in which the work of Brandt and his predecessors was fortified by her own praiseworthy efforts to grapple with a dictionary-less language. These studies were suggested, warmly encouraged and appreciated by myself, and were as follows: 'The Liberation of Jôhannâ' (*Theosophical Rev.*, Sept. 1902); 'Fragments from the Mandæan Traditions of J. the B.' (*Quest*, Ap. 1910); 'The Book of Souls: Fragments of a Mandæan Mystery Ritual' (*ib.* Jan. 1912); 'The Mandæan Chrism' (*ib.* Jan. 1914).

First let us begin with the pieces purporting to give information concerning the person of the prophet.

I.—THE GNOSTIC JOHN THE BAPTIZER.

Portents at John's Birth (§18).[1]

In the Name of Great Life may hallowed Light be glorified.

A CHILD was planted out of the height, a mystery revealed in Jerusalem.[2] The priests saw dreams; chill seized on their children, chill seized on Jerusalem.

Early in the morning he[3] went to the temple. He opened his mouth in blasphemy and his lips of lying. He opened his mouth in blasphemy and spake to all of the priests:

"In my vision of the night I beheld, [I beheld] in my vision. When I lay there, I slept not and rested not, and sleep came not to me by night. I slept not and rested not, [and I beheld] that a star appeared and stood over Enishbai.[4] Fire burned in Old Father (Abā Sābā) Zakhriā;[5] three heaven-lights appeared.[6] The

---

[1] Because Yōhānā is mentioned only once in the *Genzā*, Brandt supposes that the John-Book pieces must be later in date. But surely this is not a scientific conjecture. It is rather to be supposed that the John-pieces were naturally gathered together from the general mass of material when the collection-process began. Though Yahyā is the Arabic form of the name, Yōhānā alternates with it; this shows a later redaction in the Mohammedan period, when the people vulgarly spoke Arabic, but says nothing as to the date of earlier writings from which the pieces were copied out.

[2] *Ur-ashlam*, a mock-name or derisive caricature-permutation='Ur perfected' it. Ur is originally the Chaldæan Deus Lunus; he is the eldest son of Rūhā, the World-Mother, and corresponds in some respects with the Yaldabaōth of 'Ophite' gnosticism.

[3] Who it was is not disclosed. The dreamer's report is at first utterly discredited.

[4] The Elisabeth of Luke. The name may be some mystical echo of Elisheba, the wife of Aaron, the first priest, just as the Miriam of the Jesus birth-story reminds us of Miriam the prophetess, the sister of Moses, the first prophet. If the pre-Christian Palestinian Dorshē Reshumōth may be thought incapable of going so far, the Alexandrian Jewish allegorists, to whose school Philo belonged, would, and did, sublimate the sister or wife of a sage into a figure of his spiritual virtue or power. This will become clearer later on.

[5] The Zacharias of Luke.

[6] Cp. the more concrete three Magi motive. It should, however, be noted that Origen (1st half of 3rd cent.) is the first of the Fathers to state that the number of the Magi was 3; Chrysostom, 150 years later, gives their number as 12 (see Lynn Thorndike, *A History of Magic and Experimental Science* London, 1923, i. 472ff.).

sun sank and the lights rose. Fire lit up the house of the people (synagogue), smoke rose over the temple. A quaking quaked in the Throne-chariot,[1] so that Earth removed from her seat. A star flew down into Judæa, a star flew down into Jerusalem. The sun appeared by night, and the moon rose by day."

When the priests heard this, they cast dust on their head. Yaqif the priest weeps and Beni-Amin's tears flow.[2] Shilai and Shalbai[3] cast dust on their heads. Elizar[4] [the chief priest] opened his mouth and spake unto all of the priests: "Yaqif interprets dreams, but as yet he has no understanding of these. Beni-Amin interprets dreams; is he not a man who discloses your

---

[1] Merkabah; here presumably meaning heaven generally.

[2] The narrative is largely in the familiar style of Danielic and Talmūdic chronological camouflage; the Daniel Book (c. 164 B.C.) throws back the religio-political conflict of the Jews with the kingdom and Hellenistic religion of Antiochus Epiphanes to the days of Nebuchadrezzar (c. 600 B.C.), and the Talmūd Jesus stories, for instance, throw back the setting to some 100 years B.C. or advance it to some 100 years A.D. See my *Did Jesus Live 100 B.C.?—An Enquiry into the Talmud-Jesus Stories, the Toldoth Jeshu and Some Curious Statements of Epiphanius—Being a Contribution to the Study of Christian Origins* (London, 1903). It is to be noted that the Talmūd knows nothing of John; it evidently regards the John-Jesus movement as one and the same kind of heresy. Y. and B. may perhaps be personified types of members of certain contemporary communities or mystical groups. In §54 Y. and B. are called the 'Two Gold-sons.' This reminds us of alchemical symbolism; see my tracing of 'psychical' alchemy to Babylon in *The Doctrine of the Subtle Body in Western Tradition* (London, 1919), Proem, pp. 25ff. They may have belonged to the early ' Sons of the Sun' tradition—the later Sampsæans of Epiphanius, still later in wider distribution known to the Moslim historians as Shemsīyeh (Shamish=the Sun). This hypothesis is strengthened by the apparently cryptic gloss Beni-Amin, ' Sons of (the) Amēn' (cp. Rev. iii. 14: "These things saith the Amēn, the faithful and true witness, the beginning of the creation of God"). I have no space here to follow up this conjecture; but L. seems to me to be, not only nodding, but fast asleep, when he assumes that the Mandæan writers were simply ignoramuses who mistook Ben-Yamin for Beni-Amin. The Heb. derivation of Benjamin is given very variously in the Apocrypha and Pseudepigrapha of the O.T. L. refers to Yaqif (clearly Jacob) as Joseph.

[3] Of whom we have no further information.

[4] Can this be camouflage for Rabbi Eliazer ben Hyrcanus, the founder of the famous Rabbinical school at Lud (Lydda) and teacher of Akiba? He flourished 70-100 A.D. R. Eliazer was imprisoned for heresy; the Talmūd account connects this accusation of heresy with an interview between him and a certain Jacob of Kephar Sechania, a city in lower Galilee, who is said to have been one of the disciples of Jeshu ha-Notzri, i.e. J. the Nāzōræan (see *D.J.L. 100 B.C.?*—pp. 216ff. for reference and discussion). But Eliazer is a name of great distinction in Pharisaic priestly tradition, especially that of the Maccabæan proto-martyr priest, the teacher of the martyred Seven Sons and the Mother in *IV. Maccabees*.

secrets? Ṭāb-Yōmīn¹ gives us no revelation, though you deem he can give information on all that is and [that] is not.

Earth groans out of season and is sent a-whirl through the heaven-spheres. Earth² opens her mouth and speaks to Elizar: "Go to Lilyukh,³ that he may interpret the dreams you have seen." Thereon Elizar opened his mouth and spake unto all of the priests: "Who goes to Lilyukh, that he may interpret the dreams you have seen?" Then wrote they a letter and put it in the hand of Ṭab-Yōmīn. Ṭāb-Yōmīn took the letter and betook himself to Lilyukh. Lilyukh lay on his bed; sleep had not yet flown from him. A quaking came into his heart, shivered his heart and brought it down from its stay. Ṭāb-Yōmīn drew near to Lilyukh. Ṭāb-Yōmīn stepped up to Lilyukh, shook him out of his sleep and spake to him: "The priests saw dreams, . . . [the above paragraph is repeated verbally down to] . . . and the moon rose by day."

When Lilyukh heard this, he cast dust on his head. Naked, Lilyukh rose from his bed and fetched the dream-book. He opens it and reads in it and looks for what stands there written. He opens it and reads therein and interprets the dreams in silence without reading aloud. He writes them in a letter and expounds them on a leaf. In it he says to them: "Woe unto you, all of you priests, for Enishbai shall bear a child. Woe unto you, ye rabbis, for a child shall be born in Jerusalem. Woe unto you, ye teachers and pupils, for Enishbai shall bear a child. Woe unto you, Mistress Torah (the Law), for Yōhānā shall be born in Jerusalem."

Lilyukh writes unto them in the letter and says to them: "The star, that came and stood over Enishbai: A child will be planted out of the height from above; he comes and will be given unto Enishbai. The fire, that burned in Old Father Zakhriā: Yōhānā will be born in Jerusalem."

Ṭāb-Yōmīn took the letter and in haste made off to Jerusalem.

¹ Unidentified by L. Can it be camouflage for Tabbai, father of R. Jehuda, who was 'pair' to Simeon ben Shetach, in the Pal. Talmūd Jesus-story (*Chag.* 77d), see Mead, *op. cit.* pp. 148f.

² The source of E.'s inspiration is the Earth; the source of John's is the Sun (see below §20—p. 43).

³ This is most probably Elijah (the Eliyahū of the O.T.); I owe this illuminating conjecture to Dr. M. Gaster. Is there here also a hidden reference to an existing 'School of the Prophets'?

He came and found all the priests sitting in sorrow. He took the letter and laid it in the hand of Elizar. He (E.) opens it and reads it and finds in it wondrous discourses. He opens it and reads it and sees what stands therein written. He reads it in silence and gives them no decision about it. Elizar then took it and laid it in the hand of Old Father Zakhriā. He (Z.) opens it and reads it and sees what stands therein written. He reads it in silence and gives no decision about it. Elizar now opened his mouth and spake to Old Father Zakhriā: " Old Father, get thee gone from Judæa, lest thou stir up strife in Jerusalem." Old Father then raised his right hand and smote on the head Elizar: " Elizar, thou great house, thou head of all the priests! If thou in thy inner [part] knewest thy mother, thou wouldst not dare come into our synagogue. If thou in thy inner [part] knewest, thou wouldst not dare read the Torah. For thy mother was a wanton.[1] A wanton was she, who did not match with the house of her husband's father. As thy father had not the hundred gold staters for writing her the bill of divorcement, he abandoned her straightway and enquired not for her. Is there a day when I come and look forth,[2] and see not Mīshā bar Amrā?[3] Yea, is there a day when I come without praying in your synagogue, that you (pl.) should be false and dishonest and say a word which you have ne'er heard about me? Where is there a dead man who becomes living again, that Enishbai should bear a child? Where is there a blind man who becomes seeing, where is there a lame man for whom his feet [walk again], and where is there a mute who learns [to read in] a book, that Enishbai should bear a child? It is two and twenty years'[4] to-day that I have seen no wife. Nay, neither through me nor through you will Enishbai bear a child."

Then all of the priests arose and said to Old Father Zakhriā, [they said] in reproach: " Be at rest and keep thy seat, Old Father, and let the calm of the Good (pl.) rest upon thee. Old

[1] This is the same motive as that in the Talmūd Jesus-stories and Toldoth. It is the language of popular, Bazaar theological controversy, and is in keeping with Jewish figurative diction in which 'fornication' is the general term for all lapses from right religious beliefs and views.

[2] ? in vision.

[3] Moses, son of 'Amram.

[4] Elsewhere we learn that Zakhriā was 99 and Enishbai 88 at John's birth and that John himself began his ministry at the age of 22. A mystic psephology is here clearly employed.

Father, if there were no dreams in Judæa, then would all that Mishā has said, be lying. Rather shall thy word and our word be made good, and the dreams we have seen. Yōhānā will receive Jordan and be called prophet in Jerusalem."

Thereon Old Father removed himself from their midst, and Elizar followed him. Then were seen three lights (lit. lamps) which companied with him (Z.). They (the priests) ran up, caught Old Father by the hem of his robe and said to him: "Old Father, what is 't that goes before thee, and what is 't that follows thee?" Then answered he them: "O Elizar, thou great house, thou head of all of the priests, I know not whom the lights guard which go before me. I know not with whom the fire goes which follows me. [But] neither through me nor through you will Enishbai bear a child."

Then all the priests rose and said to Old Father Zakhriā, [they said] in reproach: "Old Father Zakhriā, be at peace, firm and decided, for the child will be planted from out of the most high height and be given to thee in thy old age. Yōhānā will be born, Yōhānā will receive Jordan and be called prophet in Jerusalem. We will be baptized with his baptizing and with his pure sign [will we] be signed. We will take his bread and drink his drink and with him ascend to Light's region."

All the priests arose and said to Old Father Zakhriā, [they said] in reproach: "Old Father! We will enlighten thee as to thy race[1] and thy fathers, from whom thou hast come forth. . . . [there follows a list of prophets and sages, beginning with Moses, which I omit, as it requires a lengthy commentary for which space here does not serve,—ending with]. . . Ṭāb-Yōmīn and the school-teachers have come forth from thy race. The blessed princes, who are thy forbears, Old Father, all of them have taken no wife and begotten no sons.[2] Yet in their old age[3] each of them

[1] *Sc.* the race of the righteous, of the spiritual or perfect. It has many names in mystical literature of the first centuries, as for instance in Philo, who distinguishes 'race' and 'kin' of God from 'people' of God. See for references and quotations my *Thrice-greatest Hermes* (London, 1906), Index *s.v.* 'Race.'

[2] The same mystic idea underlies the words of Philo about the women Therapeuts (*D.V.C.*): "Their longing is not for mortal children, but for a deathless progeny which the soul that is in love with God can alone bring forth." See my translation in *Fragments of a Faith Forgotten* (London, 2nd ed., 1906), p. 75. It is the Melchisedec motive also.

[3] The Later Platonists glossed 'old age' as used by Plato to signify the age of wisdom.

had a son.¹ They had sons, and they were prophets in Jerusalem. If now out of thee as well a prophet comes forth, thou dost then revive this race again. Yea, Yōhānā will be born and will be called prophet in Jerusalem."

Then Elizar opened his mouth and said to Old Father: "Old Father! If Yōhānā receives Jordan, then will I be his servant, be baptized with his baptizing and signed with his pure sign. We will take his bread and drink his drink and with him ascend to Light's region." Then Old Father opened his mouth and said unto all of the priests: "If the child comes out of the most high height, what then will *you* do in Jerusalem?"

They² have taken the child out of the basin of Jordan and laid him in the womb of Enishbai.

Life is victorious and victorious is the Man³ who has come hither.

JOHN'S PROCLAMATION CONCERNING HIMSELF AND HIS ASSUMPTION OF THE PROPHET'S MANTLE (§ 19).

Yahyā proclaims in the nights, Yōhānā on the Night's evenings.⁴

YAHYĀ proclaims in the nights and says:

"Through my Father's discourses I give light and through the praise of the Man, my creator. I have freed my soul from the world and from the works that are hateful and wrong. The Seven⁵ put question to me, the Dead who have not seen Life, and they say: "In whose strength dost thou stand there, and with

---

¹ The prophets are god-sons of their god-parents; father and son are the usual terms for the relationship between master and pupil in sacred things.

² That is, the heavenly messengers.

³ The Heavenly Man of Light. The Man-doctrine is an essential element of the Gnosis, as it was also with Jesus. ('Son of Man' is the Aramæan idiom for 'Man' simply.) See Reitzenstein's *Poimandres* (Leipzig, 1904), my *Thrice-greatest Hermes* (1906), and Bousset, *op. cit.* (1907), indexes.

⁴ This introductory formula, as is the case with other headings and conclusions, is due to the collectors and editors. It is unexplained, but seems to refer to the dark period before the dawn of the Day of Light which was expected. The days of *this* age are spiritual nights. *N.B.* a prophet 'proclaims,' he does not 'preach.'

⁵ This-World-rulers or Archontes, the Planets or Planetary Spirits, which the MM. regarded as evil powers. They are the 'Dead' as having no spiritual Life.

whose praise dost thou make proclamation?" Thereon I gave to them answer: "I stand in the strength of my Father and with the praise of the Man, my creator. I have built no house in Judæa, have set up no throne in Jerusalem. I have not loved the wreath of the roses, not commerce with lovely women. I have not loved the defective,[1] not loved the cup of the drunkards. I have loved no food of the body, and envy has found no place in me. I have not forgotten my night-prayer, not forgotten wondrous Jordan. I have not forgotten my baptizing, not [forgotten] my pure sign. I have not forgotten Sun-day,[2] and the Day's evening has not condemned me. I have not forgotten Shilmai and Nibdai,[3] who dwell in the House of the Mighty.[4] They clear me and let me ascend; they know no fault, no defect is in me."

When Yahyā said this, Life rejoiced over him greatly. The Seven sent him their greeting and the Twelve[5] made obeisance before him. They said to him: "Of all these words which thou hast spoken, thou hast not said a single one falsely. Delightful and fair is thy voice, and none is an equal to thee. Fair is thy discourse in thy mouth and precious thy speech, which has been bestowèd upon thee. The vesture which First Life did give unto Adam, the Man,[6] the vesture which First Life did give unto Rām,[7]

[1] A technical term—the things that 'fall short' as compared with the 'fulness' of perfection; cp. the *plērōma* and *hysterēma* of numerous Greek Gnostic documents.

[2] Brandt (Art. *E.R.E.*) apologetically conjectures that this observance of Sun-day (*hab šabbā*) was taken over from Syro-Christian usage. But reverence for Sun-day is fundamental with the MM., and it is one of their celestial personifications. The MM. loathed idolatry and sun-worship; they worshipped Life and Light, but may have venerated the light as the symbol of that Light. The same puzzle occurs with the prayer-custom of the Essenes, who turned to the rising sun in their morning orisons. The problem we have here to face is the existence of a pre-Christian Sun-day as rigidly observed as the Jews and others kept the Sabbath, and not a 'Pagan' holy-day.

[3] The twin Jordan-Watchers.

[4] *Sc.* Life.

[5] The powers of the Cosmic Animal-life Circle or Zodiac, which were held by the MM. to be equally inimical with the Seven. Both orders were sons of the World-mother Namrūs, generally called Rūhā, *i.e.* Spirit, the World-spirit, spirit here being used in the wide-spread sense of the lower, animal spirit.

[6] *Sc.* the Celestial Man or Adam of Light.

Rām the Great, coupled also with Bīhrām (presumably the Pahlavi or Later Persian form, also Bahrām=Avestan Verethragna).

the Man, the vesture which First Life did give unto Shurbai,[1] the Man, the vesture which First Life did give unto Shum bar Nū,[2]—has He given now unto thee. He hath given it thee, O Yahyā, that thou mayest ascend, and with thee may those ascend * * * * * * The house of defect[3] will be left behind in the desert.[4] Everyone who shall be found sinless, will ascend to thee to the Light's region; he who is not found sinless, will be called to account in the guard-houses."[5]

And Life is victorious.

John's Light-ship (§ 20).

Yahyā proclaims in the nights, Yōhānā on the Night's evenings.

YAHYĀ proclaims in the nights and says: "In the name of Him who is wondrous and all-surpassing! The Sun sat in his Court (? Corona), and the Moon sat in the Dragon. The Four

---

[1] Not identified.

[2] Shem, son of Noah. The first age or world-period was that of Adam; the second, of Rām and Rūd (fem.); the third, of Shurbai and Sharhab-ēl; the fourth, that of the Flood. The second generation perished by the sword and pestilence, the third by fire (cp. § 25 below). The Indian *yugas* came from the same source. As to the prophetical vesture in this special connection, apart from the more general wide-spread notion of the garment of light or robe of glory. cp. the Rabbinical tradition in the mediæval *Yaschar* or *Sepher Hai-yaschar* (*The Book of the Just*, more commonly known as *The Book of the Generations of Adam* or *The Book of the History of Man*) which contains ancient material, translated into French by Chevalier P. L. B. Drach: "After the death of Adam and Eve the coats [*sc.* of skin—see R. Eisler's brilliant conjecture that J. the B. outwardly assumed his camel's hair robe in memory of the first garments of the fallen protoplasts, as a sign of repentance, in the preceding study] were given to Enoch, son of Jared. Enoch, at the time of his being taken to God, gave them to his son Methusaleh. After the death of Methusaleh, Noah took them and hid them in the ark. Ham stole them, and hid them so successfully that his brethren were unable to find them. Ham gave them secretly to his eldest son, Chus, who made a mystery of it to his brothers and sons. When Nimrod [=Zoroaster, see Bousset, *op. cit.*, index] reached the age of 20 years, he (Chus) clothed him with this vesture, which gave him extraordinary strength" (Migne, *Dic. des Apocryphes*, ii. 1102, 1150; and see my *World-Mystery* (London, 2nd ed., 1907), § 'The Soul-Vestures,' pp. 115ff.). It would not be difficult to penetrate under the *camouflage* of the Rabbinic tradition, but space does not serve.

[3] *Sc.* the body.

[4] *Mysticè* 'this world'?

The prison-houses of the Seven and Twelve.

Winds of the House get them gone on their wings and blow not."¹

The Sun opened his mouth and spake unto Yahyā:² "Thou hast three [head-] bands [and] a crown which equals in worth the whole world. Thou hast a ship of *mashklil*,³ which sails about here on the Jordan. Thou hast a great vessel which sails about here 'twixt the waters.⁴ If thou goest to the House of the Great [One], remember us in the Great's presence." Thereon Yahyā opened his mouth and spake to the Sun in Jerusalem: "Thou enquirest about the [head-] bands, may the Perfect (pl.) watch o'er thy crown. This *mashklil*-ship they have carpentered together⁵ with glorious splendour. On the vessel that sails 'twixt the waters, the seal of the King has been set. She⁶ who in thy house⁷ plays the wanton, goes hence and approaches the dung-house;⁸ she seeks to have children from her own proper spouse,⁹ and she does not find them. If she then¹⁰ has fulfilled her vow, and she departs,¹¹ she is unworthy for the House of the Life and will not be allotted to the Light Dwelling.

And praisèd be Life.

---

¹ All was at peace, the Sun shining brightly, the Moon sunk in the darkness beneath. Cp. 'The Mystic Hymnody' at end of 'The Secret Sermon on the Mountain' (*Corp. Herm.* xiii-xiv., Mead ii. 230): "Ye Heavens open, and ye Winds stay still; [and] let God's Deathless Sphere receive my word!"

² Note that it is the Earth that speaks to Elizar (§ 18—p. 37), signifying the lower source of his inspiration.

³ Meaning not yet determined; L. thinks it means some sort of wood, but this does not seem to be very appropriate.

⁴ *Sc.* the waters above and the waters below the firmament.

⁵ For the Carpenter-motive in connection with the John-Noah hewing of the timber for the salvation-ark-building see the previous study and especially the Samaritan Midrash concerning the S. Ta'eb (Deliverer or Messiah) and the mystic ark of conversion (pp. 8 and 21f.).

⁶ A cryptic sentence referring to the 'fornicators' who are not true the True Religion of the MM.; 'she' = the soul.

⁷ That is the world-house illuminated by the Sun.

⁸ *Sc.* hell.

⁹ *Sc.* God, as in the thought-sphere of Philo's Therapeuts.

¹⁰ After renouncing heretical views.

¹¹ That is from the body.

John the Ascetic (§ 21).

Yahyā proclaims in the nights, Yōhānā on the Night's evenings.

YAHYĀ proclaims in the nights and speaks: "Stand not I here alone? I go to and fro. Where is a prophet equal to me? Who makes proclamation equal to my proclamations, and who doth discourse with my wondrous voice?"

When Yahyā thus spake, the two women weep. Miryai[1] and Enishbai weep, and for both tears flow. They say: "We will go hence, and do thou stay here; see that thou dost not bring us to stumble.—I (M.) will go hence, and do thou stay here; see that thou dost not bring me to stumble.—I (E.) will go hence, and do thou stay here; see that thou dost not fill me with sorrow."

Then Yahyā opened his mouth and spake to Enishbai in Jerusalem: "Is there any who could take my place in the height? Is there any who could take my place in the height, so that thou mayest pay for me ransom? If thou canst pay for me ransom, then bring thy jewels and ransom me. If thou canst pay for me ransom, then bring thy pearls and ransom me. If thou canst pay for me ransom, then bring thy gold and ransom me."[2]

Thereon Enishbai opened her mouth and spake to Yahyā in Jerusalem: "Who is thy equal in Judæa, who is thy equal in Jerusalem, that I should look on him and forget thee?"—"Who is my equal, who is my equal, that thou shouldst look on him and forget me? Before my voice and the voice of my proclamations the Torah disappeared in Jerusalem. Before the voice of my discourse the readers read no more in Jerusalem. The wantons cease from their lewdness, and the women go not forth to the . . . . Hither [to me] come the brides in their wreaths, and their tears flow down to the earth. The child in the womb of his mother heard my voice and did weep. The merchants trade not in Judæa,

---

[1] Miryai is the personification of the first Mand. community among the Jews. She is presumably not to be confounded in any way with Miriam, the mother of Išū Mšīhā (Jesus Messiah), who is called Miryam (not Miryai) in § 30; but this requires further investigation.

[2] 'Jewels,' 'pearls' and 'gold' are presumably the figures of spiritual riches.

and the fishers fish not in Jerusalem.¹ The women of Israel dress not in dresses of colour,² the brides wear no gold and the ladies no jewels. Women and men look no more at their face in a mirror. Before my voice and the voice of my proclamations the water rose up to the pillars.³ Because of my voice and the voice of my proclamations the fish brought to me their greetings. Before my voice and the voice of my proclamations the birds made obeisance and said: "Well for thee, and again well for thee, Yahyā, and well for the Man whom thou dost worship. Thou hast set thyself free and won thy release, O Yahyā, and left the world empty. The women have not led thee away with their lewdness, and their words have not made thee distracted. Through sweet savours and scents thou hast not forgotten thy Lord from thy mind. Thou has not made thyself drunken with wine and hast done no deeds of impiety. No backsliding has seized on thee in Jerusalem. Thou hast set thyself free and won thy release and set up thy throne for thee in Life's House."

And Life is victorious.

OF JUDGMENT-DAY (§ 25).

Yahyā proclaims in the nights, Yōhānā on the Night's evenings.

YAHYĀ proclaims and speaks: "Ye nobles, who lie there, ye ladies, who will not awaken,—ye who lie there, what will you do on the Day of the Judgment? When the soul strips off the body, on Judgment-Day what will you do? O thou distracted, jumbled-up world in ruin! Thy men die, and thy false scriptures are closed. Where is Adam, the First Man, who was here head of the

¹ The 'merchants' and 'fishers' in all probability mean the Seven, as in the 'Fisher of Souls' piece.

² The MM. wear white robes.

³ *Sc.* of the temple; cp. the miraculous spiritual outpouring of the Last Days expected by John, based on O.T. prophecies, as set forth in the previous introductory study; also one of the *Odes of Solomon*, quoted in the *Pistis Sophia* (ch. 65, pag. 131, Mead p. 110): "A stream came forth and became a great wide flood. It tore away all to itself and turned itself against the temple," etc. The whole Ode is most instructive in this connection, and the Odes in general move in a very similar atmosphere to the John-lore. (See for Trans. from Syriac, Rendel Harris and Mingana, *The Odes and Psalms of Solomon*, Manchester, 1920). The 'fish' and 'birds' of the next sentences are the faithful.

æon? Where is Hawwā (Eve), his wife, out of whom the world was awakened to life? Where is Shit-il (Seth), son of Adam, out of whom worlds and æons arose? Where is Rām and Rūd, who belonged to the Age of the Sword? Where are Shurbai and Sharhab-ēl, who belonged to the Age of the Fire? Where is Shum bar Nū (Shem, son of Noah), who belonged to the Age of the Flood? All have departed and have not returned and taken their seats as Guardians in this world.'[The Last Day] is like a feast-day, for which the worlds and the æons are waiting. The Planets are [like] fatted oxen, who stand there for the Day of the Slaughter. The children of this world are [like] fat rams, who stand in the markets for sale.[2] But as for my friends, who pay homage to Life, their sins and transgressions will be forgiven them."

And Life is victorious.

The Letter of Truth (§ 26).

[The introductory formula and beginning of this piece are missing from the MSS.]

* * * * * *

[Yōhānā is apparently speaking.]

I TAKE no delight in the æons, I take no delight in all of the worlds. I take no delight in the æons * * * * * * *
* * * * by the Letter of Truth[3] which has come hither.

They[4] took the Letter and put it in the hand of the Jews.

---

[1] Tibil; L. frequently retains this as a proper name—*e.g.* 'in the Tibil' —and alternates it with the common noun 'world.' Whether there is a distinction in the original I do not know, it seems to be simply the Heb. *tebel* (=world, earth). Where L. has Tibil, I shall render it by 'this world.'

[2] Cp. the Messianic Marriage Feast parable (Matth. xxii. 4): "My oxen and my fatlings are killed . . .: come to the marriage-feast."

[3] Kushtā is the general term for the religious ideal of the MM.; it is elastic in meaning and cannot be translated by a single rigid concept. The original sense seems to have been 'Truth,' 'Righteousness' and perhaps 'Order' (cp. the Avestan Asha and the Vedic Rita). It thus means the true religion, loyalty, trust and faith (see J.B. xvii.f.). Kushtā is fem. It is to be noted that in Avestan literature Ashi (fem.) is the heavenly impersonation of rectitude, fortune, chastity, riches (cp. *āthrā's*), and Chisti (fem.) of religious wisdom (?=gnōsis)—see M. N. Dhalla, *Zoroastrian Civilization*, New York, 1922, pp. 45, 51f., 68, 77, 84. With the frequent recurrence of the letter-symbol in M. scripture, cp. the Syriac 'Hymn of the Soul,' or 'of the Pearl,' which belongs to the same main stream of the Gnosis (see my *Hymn of the Robe of Glory*, 'Echoes from the Gnosis' series, vol. x., London, 1908).

[4] Presumably the heavenly messengers.

These open it, read in it and see that it does not contain what they would, that it does not contain what their soul wills. They took the letter and put it in the hand of Yōhānā. "Take, Rab Yōhānā," say they to him, "Truth's Letter, which has come here to thee from thy Father."¹ Yōhānā opened it and read it and saw in it a wondrous writing. He opened it and read in it and became full of life.² "This is," says he, "what I would, and this does my soul will."

Yōhānā has left his body³; his brothers make proclamations, his brothers proclaim unto him on the Mount, on Mount Karmel.⁴ They⁵ took the Letter and brought it to the Mount, to Mount Karmel. They read out of the Letter to them⁶ and explain to them the writing,—to Yaqif and Beni-Amin and Shumēl.⁷ They assemble on Mount Karmel.

* * * * * *

[What follows is presumably the beginning of the Letter.]

Gnosis of Life⁸ who is far from the height [writes]:

"I have come unto thee, O Soul, whom Life has sent into this world. In robes of the Eight⁹ went I into the world. I went in the vesture of Life and came into the world. The vesture I brought of the Seven, I went as far as the Eight. The vesture of the Seven I took and took hold of the Eight with my hand. [I have

---

¹ *Sc.* Life or perhaps rather the Man.

² This seems cryptically to refer to some Gnostic scripture prior to John.

³ *Sc.* in trance.

⁴ Ṣūfīs would at once conclude that this refers to the Dīvān, the nightly Meeting of the Perfect in spirit presided over by the Quṭb (Pillar or Axis), the Head of the age. Mt. Karmel is identified with the story of Elijah and has always continued to be a sacred mount. Doubtless communities of 'Sons of the Prophets' and the rest had continuously there their retreats. Can it be that Ṭāb Yōmīn went to Mt. Karmel to find Lilyukh (Eli-yahu)? Karmel = the Garden or Garden-land. It had been a sacred spot long before the days of Elijah, who hid there from his pursuers in its numerous grottos. The Arabs still call it Jebal Mar Elyas (Mount Lord Elijah). Yamblichus in his *Life* of the sage says that Pythagoras visited it.

⁵ *Sc.* the heavenly messengers.

⁶ *Sc.* the brethren who had equally 'left the body.'

⁷ Plainly Samuel.

⁸ Maudā d'Haiyē, the M. Saviour; he is 'far from the height' because he is the Exile, the Stranger, in this world.

⁹ The higher Ogdoad; I conjecture, therefore, that this is a more ancient piece. The John-gnosis had depressed the Eight and the Seven and Twelve to the infernals, yet retained memory of a Great Eight and the rest.

taken them] and I take them, and I will take them and not let them go. I have taken them and hold them fast, and the wicked spirits shall change into good.

"Wherefor do ye weep, generations, wherefor weep ye, O peoples? Wherefor fadeth your splendour? For you have I brought my Image, I betook myself into the world."

And Life is victorious.

JOHN'S INVULNERABILITY (§ 27).

Yahyā proclaims in the nights, Yōhānā on the Night's evenings.

YAHYĀ proclaims in the nights and speaks: "Is there any one greater than I? They measure my works; my wage is assayed and my crown, and my praise brings me on high in peace." * * *

Yaqif leaves the house of the people, Beni-Amin leaves the temple, Elizar, the great house, leaves the dome of the priests. The priests spake unto Yahyā in Jerusalem: "Yahyā, go forth from our city! Before thy voice quaked the house of the people, at the sound of thy proclamations the temple did quake, at the sound of thy discourse quaked the priests' dome." Thereon Yahyā answered the priests in Jerusalem: "Bring fire and burn me; bring sword and hew me in pieces." But the priests in Jerusalem answered to Yahyā: "Fire does not burn thee, O Yahyā, for Life's Name has been uttered o'er thee. A sword does not hew thee in pieces, O Yahyā, for Life's Son[1] rests here upon thee."

And Life is victorious.

JOHN AND THE BAPTISM OF JESUS (§ 30).

Yahyā proclaims in the nights, Yōhānā on the Night's evenings.

YAHYĀ proclaims in the nights.—Glory rises over the worlds.

Who told Yeshu (Eshu)? Who told Yeshu Messiah, son of Miryam, who told Yeshu, so that he went to the shore of the Jordan and said [unto Yahyā]: "Yahyā, baptize me with thy baptizing and utter o'er me also the Name thy wont is to utter. If I show myself as thy pupil, I will remember thee then in my writing;

---

[1] Clearly Gnosis of Life, the Son of God and Father of John.

I attest not myself as thy pupil, then wipe out my name from thy page."

Thereon Yahyā answered Yeshu Messiah in Jerusalem: "Thou hast lied to the Jews and deceived the priests. Thou hast cut off their seed from the men and from the women bearing and being pregnant. The sabbath, which Moses made binding, hast thou relaxed[1] in Jerusalem. Thou hast lied unto them with horns[2] and spread abroad disgrace with the shofar."

Thereon Yeshu Messiah answered Yahyā in Jerusalem: "If I have lied to the Jews, may the blazing fire consume me. If I have deceived the priests, a double death will I die. If I have cut off their seed from the men, may I not cross o'er the End-Sea. If I have cut off from the women birth and being pregnant, then is in sooth a judge raised up before me. If I have relaxed the sabbath, may the blazing fire consume me. If I have lied to the Jews, I will tread on thorns and thistles. If I have spread disgrace abroad with horn-blowing, may my eyes then not light on Abathur.[3] So baptize me then with thy baptizing, and utter o'er me the Name thy wont is to utter. If I show myself as thy pupil, I will remember thee then in my writing; if I attest not myself as thy pupil, then wipe out my name from thy page."

Then spake Yahyā to Yeshu Messiah in Jerusalem: "A stammerer becomes not a scholar, a blind man writes no letter. A desolate house[4] mounts not to the height, and a widow becomes not a virgin. Foul water becomes not tasty, and a stone does not with oil soften."

Thereon Yeshu Messiah made answer to Yahyā in Jerusalem: "A stammerer a scholar becomes, a blind man writes a letter. A desolate house mounts unto the height, and a widow becomes a virgin. Foul water becomes tasty, and a stone with oil softens."

Thereon spake Yahyā unto Yeshu Messiah in Jerusalem: "If

---

[1] This makes it clear that the strict observance of *a* sabbath (Sunday) by the MM. was not taken over from the Christians, as Brandt supposes.

[2] Cp. the Joshua ben Perachiah Jesus-story in the Talmūd (*B. Sanhedrin* 107b, *Sota* 47a): Joshua replied [to Jesus]: "Thou godless one, dost thou occupy thyself with such things?—directed that 400 horns should be brought and put him under strict excommunication" (Mead, *D.J.L. 100 B.C.?* pp. 137 and 146f.).

[3] The Man 'with the Scales'—the Avestan Rashnu—who weighs the good and bad deeds of the departed (J.B. xxix. f.).

[4] Generally meaning an unmarried man.

thou giv'st me illustration for this, thou art [really] a wise Messiah."

Thereon Yeshu Messiah made answer to Yahyā in Jerusalem: "A stammerer a scholar becomes: a child who comes from the bearer, blooms and grows big. Through wages and alms he comes on high; he comes on high through wages and alms, and ascends and beholds the Light's region.

"A blind man who writes a letter: a villain who has become virtuous. He abandoned wantonness and abandoned theft and reached unto faith in almighty Life.

"A desolate house who ascends again to the height: one of position who has become humble. He quitted his palaces and quitted his pride and built a house on the sea[-shore]. A house he built on the sea[-shore], and into it opened two doors, so that he might bring in unto him whoever lay down there in misery,—to him he opened the door and took him within to himself. If he would eat, he laid for him a table with Truth. If he would drink, he mixed for him [wine-]cups [with Truth]. If he would lie down, he spread a bed for him in Truth. If he would depart, he led him forth on the way of Truth. He led him forth on the way of Truth and of faith, and then he ascends and beholds the Light's region.

"A widow who a virgin becomes: a woman who already in youth has been widowed. She kept her shame closed, and sat there till her children were grown.[1] If she passes over, her face does not pale in her husband's[2] presence.

"Foul water that is made tasty: a girl wanton who has got back her honour: she went up a hamlet and she went down a hamlet without taking her veil from her face.

"A stone with oil softens: a heretic who has come down from the mountain.[3] He abandoned magic and sorcery and made

[1] Presumably her spiritual children.

[2] Meaning God.

[3] L. thinks that by zandīq (heretic) is meant a Zoroastrian or Manichæan who comes down from the mountains to join the Mandæans who live in the plains. This seems to me entirely mistaken. The Z.'s and M.'s lived as well on plains as on mountains. In every probability it means the Mount of Darkness on which the Seven assemble to plot against the righteous. The Seven are the lords of all the false religions. For the Mount of Hades, the Prison Mount of the Underworld in Bab. tradition, see my paper 'New-found Fragments of a Babylonian Mystery-play and the Passion-story,' Quest, Jan. 1922, p. 173.

confession to almighty Life. He found a fatherless and filled him full and filled full the widow's pockets.

"Therefor baptize me, O Yahyā, with thy baptizing and utter o'er me the Name thy wont is to utter. If I show myself as thy pupil, I will remember thee in my writing; if I attest not myself as thy pupil, then wipe out my name from thy page. Thou wilt for thy sins be haled to account, and I for my sins will be haled to account."

When Yeshu Messiah said this, there came a Letter out of the House of Abathur: "Yahyā, baptize the deceiver in Jordan. Lead him down into the Jordan and baptize him, and lead him up again to the shore, and there set him."

Then Rūhā[1] made herself like to a dove and threw a cross[2] over the Jordan. A cross she threw over the Jordan and made its water to change into various colours.[3] "O Jordan," she says, "thou sanctifiest me and thou sanctifiest my seven sons."

[Then follows what, from its animadversion on Christian institutions and especially on the use of the crucifix, is plainly a later addition. Rūhā is apparently still speaking; she is the Mother of all heresies.]

"The Jordan in which Messiah Paulis[4] was baptized, have I made into a 'trough.'[5] The bread which Messiah Paulis receives,

---

[1] The Lower Spirit, the This-World-Mother.

[2] *Sc.* of light; cp. the great light that shone on Jordan at the baptizing of Jesus in 'The Gospel according to the Hebrews.' Tatian's *Diatessaron* (Syriac, 2nd half of 2nd cent.) also preserves this feature. Bar Salibi († 1171) glosses this as follows: "And immediately, as the Gospel of the Diatessaron testifies, a mighty light flashed upon Jordan and the river was girdled with white clouds, and there appeared his many hosts that were uttering praise in the air; and Jordan stood still from its flowing, though its waters were not troubled, and a pleasant odour therefrom was wafted." There is a strong Mandæan flavour about this gloss, which doubtless rested on early tradition. See F. C. Burkitt, *Evangelion da-Mepharreshe* (Cambridge, 1904), ii. 115. This is the Christian and not the M. 'cross,' as *e.g.* used in the baptismal ceremony, which is made of a number of long sticks or wands, the ends of which are stuck in the ground and the tops crossed one over the other to represent rays of light.

[3] The Jordan is white for the MM.; the various colours signify heresies.

[4] L. thinks that this stands for Paul, and this is very probably so. But at the same time he informs us that 'Paulus,' as Lorsback has shewn, is the equivalent of a Persian word meaning 'Deceiver.' It therefore may mean simply the Messiah Deceiver.

[5] Evidently a 'font.'

have I made into a 'sacrament.' The drink which Messiah Paulis receives, have I made into a 'supper.' The head-band [which Messiah Paulis receives, have I made into a 'priest-hood.'¹ The staff which Messiah Paulis receives, have I made into a 'dung [-stick].'"²

[? Gnosis of Life speaks (cp. § 29) :]

"Let me warn you, my brothers, let me warn you, my belovèd! Let me warn you, my brothers, against the . . . who are like unto the cross. They lay it on the walls; then stand there and bow down to the block. Let me warn you, my brothers, of the god which the carpenter has joinered together. If the carpenter has joinered together the god, who then has joinered together the carpenter?"

Praisèd be Life, and Life is victorious.

(For those who are not familiar with the atmosphere of bitter inner and outer theological strife of the times, it is as well to note that the last two pieces are in the form of *haggadic* controversy between the *followers* of John and Jesus respectively.)

JOHN'S MARRIAGE (§ 31).

Yahyā proclaims in the nights, Yōhānā on the Night's evenings.

YAHYĀ proclaims in the nights and speaks: "The [heavenly] wheels and chariots³ quaked. Sun and Moon weep and the eyes of Rūhā⁴ shed tears."

He⁵ says: "Yahyā, thou art like to a scorched mountain, which brings forth no grapes in this world. Thou art like to a dried-up stream, on whose banks no plants are raised. Thou hast become a land without a lord, a house without worth. A false

---

The original suggests a head-covering.

We should have expected 'crosier.' Is there word-play in all these terms?

The celestial spheres.

The World-Mother-Spirit.

Who, is not clear; perhaps Gnosis of Life, the M. Saviour.

prophet hast thou become, who hast left no one to remember thy name. Who will provide thee with provision, who with victuals, and who will follow to the grave after thee?"

When Yahyā heard this, a tear gathered in his eye; a tear in his eye gathered, and he spake: "It would be pleasant to take a wife, and delightful for me to have children. But only if I take no woman,—and then comes sleep, desire for her seizes me and I neglect my night-prayer. If only desire does not wake in me, and I forget my Lord out of my mind. If only desire does not wake in me, and I neglect my prayer every time."

When Yahyā said this, there came a Letter from the House of Abathur: "Yahyā, take a wife and found a family, and see that thou dost not let this world come to an end. On the night of Monday and on the night of Tuesday go to thy first[1] bedding. On the night of Wednesday and on the night of Thursday devote thyself to thy hallowed praying. On the night of Friday and on the night of Saturday go to thy first bedding. On the night of Sunday and (? yea) on the night of the Day devote thyself to thy hallowed praying. On Sunday take three and leave three, take three and leave three.[2] See that thou dost not let the world come to an end."

Thereon they[3] fashioned for Yahyā a wife out of thee, thou Region of the Faithful.[4] From the first conception were Handan and Sharrath born. From the middle conception were Birhām and R'himath-Haiyē born. From the last conception were Nṣab, Sām, Anhar-Zīwā ⟨and Sharrath⟩ born.[5] These three conceptions took place in thee, thou Ruins, Jerusalem.

Yahyā opened his mouth and spake to Anhar in Jerusalem:

---

[1] That is, after the marriage-ceremony.

[2] This is unexplained. Lidzbarski thinks it means three baths; but more probably it means three hours for sleep and three hours for prayer, and these again repeated.

[3] Presumably the Divine Powers.

[4] That is, those faithful to Truth. It refers to the M. Abode of the Blessed, Mshunē Kushṭā. She is thus the personified Mother of the wife of Yahyā.

[5] These are elsewhere mostly names of heavenly beings and are in part to be paralleled with the children of Eve (Hawwā) in the *Genzā* (R. 108). Handan is otherwise unknown. Shar-rath may be Shar, who is elsewhere called " the great, hidden First Vine, who bears a thousand times a thousand fruits and ten thousand times ten thousand shoots." Bihrūm is a later form of the Avestan Verethragna; he is generally called 'the Great.' R'himath-

"Instruct thy daughter, that she may not perish; and I will enlighten my sons and teach [them], that they may not be hindered." Thereon Anhar opened her mouth and spake to Yahyā in Jerusalem. "I have borne sons in this world," said she to him, "yet have I not given birth to [their] heart' in the world. If they let themselves be instructed, then will they ascend to Light's region; if they let not themselves be instructed, then will the blazing fire consume them."

JOHN ON HIS OWN PASSING (§ 31 CONTD.).

Yahyā opened his mouth and spake to Anhar in Jerusalem: "If I leave the world, tell me, what wilt thou do after me?"—"I will not eat and will not drink," she answered him, "until I see thee again."—"A lie hast thou spoken, Anhar, and thy word has come forth in deception. If a day comes and a day goes, thou eatest and drinkest and forgettest me out of thy mind. I asked thee rather, by Great Life and by the eve of the Day whose name is dear: If I leave the world, tell me, what wilt thou do after me?"—"I will not wash and I will not comb me," says she to him, "until I see thee again."—"Again hast thou spoken a lie and thy word has come forth in deception. If a month comes and a month goes, thou washest and combest thee and forgettest me out of thy mind. Again did I ask thee, Anhar, by the first bed in which we both lie: If I leave my body, tell me, what wilt thou do after me?"—"I will put on no new garments," she answers him, "until I see thee again."—"Again hast thou spoken

---

Haiyē = the Living or Life's R. In the *Qolastā* or Liturgies there is a R'hum-Hai twice mentioned; he is 'Life's Beloved,' one of the four Sons of Light, or alternately of Salvation. Nṣab is elsewhere (§ 4. 8) called N. Zīwā, that is Radiant N.; he is regarded as the Great Watcher (§ 9), and his name means 'Planter,' 'Fashioner.' Sām is also called S.-Haiyē. S. the Living; he too is 'Watcher of the æons' (G. R. 313, 12ff.), and his name means 'Stablisher.' Anhar-Zīwā or the Radiant A. is feminine (cp. § 69, 7); the name might possibly remind us of the Zoroastrian Anāhitā. Anaïtis. Anhar is elsewhere called the 'Hidden Light,' and her name means 'Lightener.' Can she then have any connection with the Iexai or Yechai, the complement of Elxai (the 'Hidden Power'), mentioned by Epiphanius? The muddled-up account of the Elchasæans in the heresiological Fathers seems to me to have a close connection with Mandæan notions (see my *D. J. L. 100 B.C. ?*—ch. xviii, 'Concerning the Book of Elxai,' pp. 365-387 (London, 1903), and Brandt's study, *Elchasai: ein Religionsstifter und sein Werk* (Leipzig, 1912). The second Sharrath is evidently a doublet.

That is, spiritual sense.

a lie, Anhar, and thy word has come forth in deception. If a year comes and a year goes, thou puttest new garments on thee and forgettest me out of thy mind."

"Why dost thou not tell me all, Yahyā," says she to him; "and how sorely thou bruisest the whole of my body! If thou dost depart, when wilt thou return, that my eyes may fall upon thine?"—"If a woman in labour descends into Sheōl[1] and a bell is hung up for her in the graveyard. If they paint a picture in Sheōl, and she then goes forth and they give a feast in the graveyard. If a bride parades round in Sheōl, and they celebrate marriage in the graveyard. If the wedding-companions borrow in Sheōl, and the paying-back takes place in the graveyard."[2]

Then answered she him: "My lord, how shall it be that a woman in labour . . . " [and so on, repeating the above].

"If thou knowest," he makes answer unto her, "that this does never happen, why dost thou press me with asking: When dost thou return? I go hence and return not. Happy the day when thou dost still see me. If there were a going-away and returning, then would no widow be found in this world. If there were a going-away and returning, then would no fatherless be found in the world. If there were a going-away and returning, then no Nazōræans would be found in the world."

Thereon Anhar opened her mouth and spake to Yahyā in Jerusalem: "I will buy thee for dear gold a brick grave[3] and have a boxing of wood[4] joinered together for thee in the graveyard." But Yahyā opened his mouth and spake to Anhar in Jerusalem: "Why wilt thou buy a brick grave for dear gold and have a boxing of wood joinered for me in the graveyard? Art sure that I am

[1] That is, dies.

[2] It was the popular custom apparently, which, however, the Mandæans did not follow, when a woman was in labour, to ring a bell to ward off evil influences (cp. the Egyptian sistrum); and a picture (or pantacle) also, with a similar apotropaic purpose, was painted. If the birth was successful, a birth-feast was given. It was also the custom, when bride and groom were poor, for their friends to borrow money or go bail for the expenses of the wedding-festivities.

[3] L. prefers to translate this as 'vault,' but he seems to me to miss the meaning and that too in face of his own note, where he admits that the first word simply means 'brick.'

[4] Both references seem to refer to Egyptian motives in burial customs. For the extraordinarily interesting deduction to be made from this hint in connection with a striking phrase in one of the following Miryai-pieces (§ 35) see the note appended there (p. 69, n. 3).

returning, that thou dost say: No dust shall fall on him? Instead of buying a brick grave for dear gold, go rather and share out for me bread. Instead of getting a boxing joinered together, go rather and read for me masses for the departed."

Thereon Anhar opened her mouth and spake to Yahyā in Jerusalem: "Thou dost go hence and forget me, and I shall be cut off in the Sinners' Dwelling."[1]

[But Yahyā answered her:] "If I forget thee, may the Light Dwelling forget me. If I forget thee, may my eyes not fall on Abathur. If I ascend to Life's House, thy wailing will arise in the graveyard."

Praisèd be Life, and Life is victorious.

JOHN'S BIRTH, UPBRINGING AND FIRST APPEARANCE (§ 32).

Yahyā proclaims in the nights, Yōhānā on the Night's evenings.

YAHYĀ proclaims in the nights and speaks: "The [heavenly] wheels and chariots quaked. Earth and Heaven weep and the tears of the Clouds flow down."

"My father," says Yahyā, "was ninety and nine and my mother eighty and eight years old. Out of the basin of Jordan they[2] took me. They bore me up and laid me in the womb of Enishbai. 'Nine months,' said they, 'thou shalt stay in her womb, as do all other children.'[3] No wise woman,"[4] said he, "brought me into the world in Judæa, and they have not cut my cord in Jerusalem. They made for me no picture of lies, and for me hung up no bell of deceit.[5] I was born from Enishbai in the region of Jerusalem."

The region of Jerusalem quakes and the wall of the priests rocks. Elizar, the great house, stands there and his body trembles. The Jews gather together, come unto Old Father Zakbriā and they speak to him: "O Old Father Zakhriā, thou art to have a son. Tell us now, what name shall we give him? Shall we give

---

[1] That is the Dwelling of the Seven Rulers, and therefore this world.
[2] *Sc.* the heavenly messengers.
[3] This is perhaps to guard against docetism.
[4] Presumably = midwife.
[5] See above § 31,—p. 55, n. 2.

him for name 'Yaqif of Wisdom,' that he may teach the Book in Jerusalem? Or shall we give him for name 'Zatan the Pillar,'[1] so that the Jews may swear by him and commit no deceit?"

When Enishbai heard this, she cried out and she said: "Of all these names which you name, will I not give him one; but the name Yahyā-Yōhānā will I give him, [the name] which Life's self has given unto him."

When the Jews heard this, they were filled with wicked anger against her and said: "What weapon shall we make ready for [a certain] one[2] and his mother, that he be slain by our hand?"

When Anōsh,[3] the treasure,[4] heard this he took the child and brought it to Parwan, the white mountain, to Mount Parwan, on which sucklings and little ones on holy drink are reared up.[5]

[There I remained] until I was two and twenty years old.[6] I learned there the whole of my wisdom and made fully my own the

---

[1] Zatan-Esṭūnā, a name found also in § 35—p. 67.

[2] Jesus is sometimes in the Talmūd referred to simply as 'a certain one' or 'that one.'

[3] Enoch.

[4] *Uthra* (*ūtrā*) is a frequently occurring general term in Mandæan, of which the precise meaning has not yet been determined; L. leaves it untranslated. *Uthra* means literally 'Riches,' 'Wealth'; and may very well then stand for the notion of Treasure. It might even convey the idea of Fulness (Gk. *Plērōma*), but this is hazardous. The difficulty with Treasure is that there are also two technical M. terms for Treasure, Treasury or Treasure-house (*sc.* of Life, cp. § 57, forewords). *Uthra* seems sometimes to equate with Angel; but again this has a term for itself (*malaka*). In any case it means a heavenly or spiritual being, excarnate or incarnate, and therefore the phrase signifies the Heavenly or Spiritual Enoch. See L.'s dissertation, '*Uthra und Malaka*,' in *Orientalische Studien Theodor Nöldeke zum siebzigsten Geburtstag (12 Marz, 1906) gewidmet* (Giessen, 1906), pp. 537-545.

[5] Cp. with the above threat of killing and the removal of the child the 'Slaughter of the Innocents' and the 'Flight into Egypt' motives of the parallel Christian stories. The 'little ones' is elsewhere found frequently in Mandæan as a technical term for the initiates of the community. The sacred drink, the *mambūhā* of the M. 'eucharist,' doubtless throws back to the Mazda-yasnian *haōma*. Parwan is mentioned only in this passage. It may, however, be a clerical error; for occasionally mention is made of a land called the 'pure Tarwan.' Or is it Mt. Karmel?

[6] The numbers 99, 88, and 22 seem to belong to some system of mystic psephology, or *gematria* as the Kabalists afterwards called it. Cp. the 888 value of the name of Christ in the second-century system of the Gnostic Markos and the 666 of the Beast in the Apocalypse. I would suggest, though with hesitation, that 10's, 100's and 1000's represent 'powers,' *i.e.* so-called higher or wider planes of activity or development, and digits certain fundamental characteristics. In this connection it is of interest to note that such numbers as 1111, 2222, occur in classical Pythagorean psephology.

whole of my discourse. They clothed me with vestures of glory and veiled me with cloud-veils.[1] They wound round me a girdle,[2] of [living] water a girdle, which shone beyond measure and glistened. They set me within a cloud, a cloud of splendour, and in the seventh hour of a Sunday they brought me to the Jerusalem region. Then cried a voice in Judæa, a crying proclaimed in Jerusalem. They call out: "What woman had a son, who then was stolen? What woman has made for him a vow[3] and been heedless about it? What woman had a son, who was stolen? Let her come and see after her son."

Who told Battai, who instructed Battai, who told Battai to go and say to Enishbai: "A youth has come to Judæa, a prophet come to Jerusalem. A youth has come to Judæa; his guardian angel stands by him. His mouth is like thee and his lips [like] his father, Old Father Zakhriā. His eyes are like thee and his brows [like] his father, Old Father Zakhriā. His nose is like thee and his hands [like] his father, Old Father Zakhriā."

When Enishbai heard this, she hurried out veil-less. When Old Father Zakhriā saw her thus, he wrote her a bill of divorcement. The Sun down-murmured from heaven and the Moon from its place mid the stars. The Sun opened his mouth and spake to Old Father Zakhriā in Jerusalem: "Old Father Zakhriā, thou great dotard (?), who has grown old and lost his wits, like an Arab whom his *kismet* has forsaken.[4] A youth has come to Judæa, a prophet come to Jerusalem. A youth has come to Judæa; why dost thou send Enishbai away?"

When the youth saw her alone, he set himself free and fell down from the cloud. He set himself free and fell down from the cloud and kissed the mouth of Enishbai. When Anōsh, the treasure, saw him [do this], he spake unto Yahyā in Jerusalem: "Stands it for thee written in thy book, is it declared unto thee

---

[1] This is a reference to the heavenly cloud or surround; *e.g.* Enoch dwells in a cloud and from its matter fashions the body in which he appears upon earth or elsewhere in man-form.

[2] This spiritual girdle is symbolized by the M. sacred cord of 60 threads; cp. the Parsī cord or *kustī*, composed of 72 strands and wound three times round the body, and also the Brāhmanical sacred thread.

[3] Presumably before his birth, and perhaps dedicating him to God as a Nazīr.

[4] This phrase is most probably a late interpolation.

on thy page, to kiss her alone, on the mouth?"—Thereon answered Yahyā and spake unto Anōsh, the treasure, in Jerusalem: "Nine months I abode in her womb,[1] so long as all other children abide there, without any reluctance on her part; therefore is it no charge against me now to kiss her alone, on the mouth. Nay, hail and again hail to the man who repays father and mother in full. A man who recompenses father and mother, has not his like in the world."

When Yahyā said this, Anōsh, the treasure, knew that Yahyā is wise. Thereon Anōsh, the treasure, spake to the Sun in Jerusalem: "Take for me care of the youth, the Man, who is sent by the King. Take for me care of the youth, until we ask for him." Then Anōsh, the treasure, spake to the Moon in Jerusalem: "Take for me care of the youth, the Man, who is sent by the King. Take for me care of the youth, until we ask for him."

Life is exalted and is victorious, and victorious is the Man who has come hither.

JOHN'S ANSWER TO JESUS CONCERNING THE ANGEL OF DEATH (§ 33).

Yahyā proclaims in the nights, Yōhānā on the Night's evenings.

YAHYĀ proclaims and speaks: "Stand I not alone? Because of my voice the [heavenly] wheels quake and the chariots capsize. The tempest became silent and settled down in the world's deserts. Sun and Moon wail, and Earth and Heaven mourn."

Messiah opened his mouth and spake to Yahyā in Jerusalem:

[1] Cp. *Pistis Sophia* (p. 115; Mead², p. 97), where Jesus is made to say to his mother: "Thou, also, Mary, hast received form which is in Barbēlō [the Great Mother], according to matter, and hast received likeness which is in the Virgin of Light, according to light . . . ; and on thy account the darkness hath arisen, and moreover out of thee did come forth the material body in which I am, which I have purified and refined." Again (p. 120; M. p. 100): "Mary, my mother according to matter, thou in whom I have sojourned." And again, Mary speaking (p. 123; M. p. 103): "'Grace and Truth met together,'—it is I, Mary, thy mother, and Elizabeth, mother of John, whom I have met. 'Grace' then is the power of Sabaōth in me, which went forth out of me, which thou art. . . . . 'Truth' on the other hand is the power in Elizabeth, which is John, who did come and hath made proclamation concerning the way of Truth [the M. *Kushṭā*] which thou art,—who hath made proclamation before thee."

"I asked thee, Yahyā, by Great Life and by Sunday, whose name is dear. I asked thee Yahyā, by the Way, whereby the Men of piety put to the test go without hindrance. Tell me: To what is the shape of Ṣauriēl's[1] knife like? Tell me: If the soul leaves the body, with what is it clothed, and to what is it like in the vain body? Surely the soul is not possibly like the blood, that it should become heated in the body and come to a stop in it? Surely the soul is not possibly like the wind, that it should fare to the mountains, be lost there and come to a stop? Surely the soul is not possibly like the dew, that it should fall on the fruit and be lost?"

When Messiah said this, Yahyā cries aloud; tears come to him without ceasing, and he speaks: "[God] forbid that the high King of Light should look for lot in deceivers. The soul is not like the blood, that it should become heated in the body and come to a stop. The soul is not like the dew, that it should fall on the fruit and be lost. The soul is not like the wind, that it should fare to the mountains and come to a stop. Firmly developed has the soul been brought into the vain body. If the soul has kept herself perfect, she ascends in a garment of glory.

"Ṣauriēl's knife consists of three flames.[2] When he (Ṣ) drives her (the soul) to hasten, so as to bear her away, he lets loose the three flames against her. One he lets loose against her in the evening, the other at cock-crow; the third lets he loose 'gainst her at the coming-forth of the rays. If the fire begins to be fierce, the soul slips out of the feet and the knees. Out of the feet and the knees slips she, and draws nigh to the hips. Thereon leaves she the hips, reaches the heart, and seeks to keep there her ground. Then falls she into the breast, and it squeezes . . . . . . The eyes, the face and the lips of the man twitch, and the tongue twists hither and thither.

"Then Ṣauriēl sits on the eyebrows; [he sits] and speaks to her: 'Go hence, O Soul! Why dost thou still watch over the body?'—Then says she to him: 'Thou wilt hale me, Ṣauriēl, out of the body. First show me my vesture [and clothe me therewith]; then hale me out and hence bring me.'—'First bring me

---

[1] The Angel of Death, as with the Jews. Cp. the knife, sword or scymytar of the Ophite Diagram in Origen's reply to Celsus.

[2] Cp. the flaming sword of the Hebrew form of the Paradise-myth.

thy works and thy wage,' makes he answer to her; 'then will I show thee thy vesture and clothe thee.'—'I knew not, O Ṣauriēl,' says she to him, 'that my time is come, and they then send quickly for me, for doing good works, so that thou mayest bring me my vesture and clothe me therewith.'—Natheless he made answer unto her: 'Has no one yet died before thee and have they not yet carried forth anyone to the graveyard?'—Thereon she says to him: 'Through the power of him who has died before me, and through the power of him whom they have carried forth to the graveyard'[1] . . . .

"'[The women] who wept ran hither and thither and [the men] who wailed ran hither and thither, as long as the body lay there before them. When the soul leaves the body, four[2] go forth to the graveyard. [The women] who wept ran hither and thither, the men who wailed ran hither and thither; and they ran hither and thither crying, until they lowered it into the pit. When they had lowered the vain body and covered it over [sc. with earth], then the women ceased from their death-wail. They filled up the pit, and the men went away.. . . . . . . In haste left they the body and grave and went away; they took hold of cup and ate bread and forgot the vain body.—Now, an thou wilt, Ṣauriēl, let me stay here still two days. Then will I sell the whole of my goods and share out among my sons, and will take my vesture with me, the robe that ascends to Light's region.'

"Natheless Ṣauriēl returned answer unto her: 'Is there a child that has left the womb of its mother, and that they shall have brought back again into its mother, that I should leave thee in the Wicked Ones'[3] Dwelling, so that thou mayest see after a sharing among thy sons? I will lead thee hence and put the robe of darkness upon [thee], for that thou hast not let thyself be warnèd in this world, and hast not loved thy way to Light's region. Therefore shalt thou be put in ward in the House of the Wicked, till Heaven and Earth pass away.'"

And praisèd be Life.

[1] Here something seems to have fallen out. The following recital of the soul describes a burial which has taken place.

[2] Unexplained; it may possibly mean two female and two male professional mourners.

[3] Sc. the Seven Rulers.

II.—THE STORY OF THE BREACH WITH JUDAISM.

MIRYAI IS EXPELLED FROM JEWRY (§ 34).

In the Name of Great Life, may hallowed Light be glorified.

MIRYAI am I, of the Kings of Babel[1] a daughter, a daughter of Jerusalem's mighty rulers. They have given me birth; the priests brought me up. In the fold of their robe they carried me up into the dark house, into the temple. Adonai laid a charge on my hands and on my two arms: I must scour and cleanse the house [that is] without firmness. There is naught therein for supporting the poor, naught to revive the tormented souls.

My father went to the house of the people, my mother went to the temple. My father went out and said to me, and my mother went out and charged me: " Miryai, close thy inner doors and bolt the bar. See that thou goest not forth into the main streets and that the suns of my Lord[2] fall not upon thee."

But I, Miryai, listened not to what my mother did tell me, and hearkened not with the ear to what my father did charge me. I opened the inner doors, and the outer let I stand open. Out went I into the main streets and the suns of *my* Lord fell upon me. To the house of the people would I not go, but my way bore me unto the temple [*sc.* of the Mandæans]. I went and I found my brothers and sisters, how they stand and carry on proclamations. My brothers carry on proclamations and my sisters throw out explanations.[3] With the voice of their proclamations and with the voice of their explanations I became drowsy and laid me down on the spot.[4] My brothers went forth and did not wake me, and my sisters withdrew and roused me not. But thou, my sister in Truth,[5] dost rouse me from sleep and dost say: " Arise, arise, Miryai, before the day breaks and the cock lets crow his morn-call, before the sun shines and his glory rises over the

---

[1] A by-name for Jerusalem.

[2] Presumably Adonai; M.'s Lord is (below) the King of Light and later on her Lord is Gnosis of Life.

[3] Cp. the prophesyings and interpretations of Early Christendom and the 'glossolaly' of the earliest Pauline communities.

[4] M. became entranced. [5] Presumably a heavenly visitant.

worlds, before the priests and the priests' sons go forth and sit them down in the shade of the Ruins—Jerusalem, before thy father comes and brings upset upon thee such as thou never hast had."

I, Miryai, keep secret my prayers and utterly secret keep my discourses.

Early, day began to dawn, early the cock let crow his call, early the sun shone and his glory rose over the worlds. The priests and priests' sons went out and sat them down in the shade of the Ruins—Jerusalem. Then came my bodily father and brought on me upset such as I never have had. He spake:

"Where hast come from, thou debauched trough, whom [? locks] and bars [cannot keep in]? Where hast thou come from? Woe [unto thee], thou bitch in heat, who [? mindest] not [door-]pins and lockings! Where hast thou come from? Woe, woe [unto thee], thou bit of coarse stuff that has been patched on my robe!"

"If I am a debauched trough, I will burst thy [boltings] and bars. If I am a bitch in heat, I will draw back the pins and the lockings. If I am a bit of coarse stuff that has been patched on thy robe, then out of thy robe cut and rip me."

Thereon he cried: "Come (pl.), look on Miryai, who has left Jewry and gone to make love with her lord. Come, look on Miryai, who has left off coloured raiment and gone to make love with her lord. She forsook gold and silver and went to make love with her lord. She forsook the phylacteries[1] and went to make love with the man with the head-band."[2]

Then Miryai makes answer unto him: "Far lies it from me to love him whom I have hated. Far lies it from me to hate him whom I have loved. Nay, far from me lies it to hate my Lord, the Life's Gnosis, who is for me in the world a support. A support is he in the world for me and a helper in the Light's region. Dust in the mouth of the Jews, ashes in the mouth of all of the priests! May the dung that is under the feet of the horses, come on the high ones and Jerusalem's mighty rulers."

Life is exalted and is victorious, and victorious is the Man who has come hither.

[1] *Ṭuṭiftā*=Heb. *tefillīm*.
[2] Cp. § 22, 'the pure *burzinqā*,' and J. B., pp. 30¹ and 50.¹

A Variant of the Above from the Oxford MS. (L.'s J. B., pp. 123-125).

In the name of Great Life, may hallowed Light be glorified.

AT the door of the house of the people her mother came upon Miryai. Her mother came upon Miryai and put question to her: "Whence com'st thou, my daughter, Miryai, whose face gathers roses? Roses gathers thy face and of sleep are thy eyes full. Full of sleep are thy eyes, and upon thy forehead lies slumber."

Thereon she made answer: "It is two,—three days to-day that my brothers sat down in the house of my Father. In my Father's house sat down my brothers and let wonderful proclamations be heard. Because of the voice and the ringing of the proclamation of the treasures, my brothers, there comes no sleep over my eyes. Sleep comes not over my eyes, nor slumber upon my forehead."

"Hast thou not heard, Miryai, my daughter, what the Jews are saying about thee? The Jews are saying: Thy daughter has fallen in love with a man. She has gotten hate against Jewry and love for Nazoræanity. Hate has she gotten against the house of the people and love for the door of the temple (sc. of the MM.). Hate has she gotten against the phylacteries and love for the flaunting wreaths. Work does she on Sabbath; on Sunday she keeps her hands still. Miryai has cast aside straightway the Law that the Seven have laid [upon us]."

As Miryai stands there, she puts dust on her feet, and speaks: "Dust in the mouth of the Jews and ashes in the mouth of all of the priests! May the dung that lies under the horses, come on the elders who are in Jerusalem! I cannot hate him whose love I have won, nor love him 'gainst whom I have gotten hate. Yea, I have won the love of my Lord the Life's Gnosis, [and hope] that in him a helper will for me arise, a helper and a support from the region of Darkness unto Light's region."

Thou hast won the victory, Gnosis of Life, and helped all thy friends to victory.

And Life is victorious.

THE EXILED COMMUNITY SETTLE ON THE EUPHRATES (§ 35).

In the Name of Great Life, may hallowed Light be glorified.

MIRYAI am I, a vine, a tree, who stands at the mouth of Eu-phrates (Frash). The tree's leaves are precious stones, the tree's fruits pearls. The vine-tree's foliage is glory, its shoots precious light. Among the trees its scent it diffuses, and it spreads over all the worlds. The birds of the air scented it; a flock settled down on the tree. A flock on it down-settled, and they would build their nest there. They flutter about in it and settle not down in it firmly. Of its foliage they eat . . from its inner part they drink wine. They eat what is not to be cast away, and drink what was not wine.[1]

While the birds sat on the vine, winds and tempests broke loose. They shook the good birdlets awake, they smote 'gainst the tree; on all sides they scattered the leaves of the vine-tree and scared the birds out of their place. Many a bird there was who flew not away, but held on fast with claws and with wings, till the winds and the tempests were over. Many again held not on fast and were hurried away . . . . Woe unto those who did not hold fast, but were dashed from the tree and flew off. How fair is the tree of Life and fair the birds who dwell on it!

The winds and the tempests passed and rest came over the world.

As the birds sit there and chirp and would be a-building their nest, as the birds sit on the vine, an eagle wheeled and flew hither. A white eagle-bird[2] came, looked down and caught sight of the birds. Round wheeled he, sped down on them with his wings, and came and sat on the tree. In converse with him joined the birds, and said to him:

"By thy Life, Eagle! On this tree were we birds without number.—But there broke loose against them the winds, and on the tree came raging tempests. They shook them off from the tree, so that they tore their wings from them [nearly]. Many a one held fast, whom the winds and tempests could not tear away; but many a one flew off at top speed.—We speak to thee, therefore,

[1] The whole description is intentionally symbolic or allegorical.
[2] The White Eagle is manifestly Gnosis of Life.

O Eagle, we ask thee respecting the birds, because thou art sharp of sight and dost see all in this world: What have the winds and the tempests done with those birds, our brothers? What spyest thou out (?) over them?"

Then made he answer unto them: "You had better not to have known, my brothers, what has become of those birds. Sling-shots drove them far from me; their wings broke; torn off were they, broken off; they went hence and relied on the bird-catchers.[1] The harrier and hawk wheeled round them, tore pieces out of their flesh and fed on those who were fat. Woe to those who fell prey to the water,[2] if there was no portion for them at the crossing. Well for you, ye birds, who hold fast to this vine [here]; you became a companionship of Miryai, the vine, who stands at the mouth of Euphrates. See and satisfy yourselves, ye birds, that I have come to you. I have come to my brothers to be a support for them in this world. I have come to heal Miryai, [come] to bring water to the good, beloved plants, to the vines, who stand at the mouth of Euphrates. In a white[3] pail I draw water and bring it to my plants. I bear and I hold [it] on the arms of glory which are my own. I bear and I hold [it] and give [them] to drink. Well for him who has drunk of my water. He drinks, finds healing and confirmation, and grows to double [his stature]. The vines who drank water, brought forth good fruit. Their leaves turned on high and made a brave show. The branches which drank no water, brought forth bitter herbs and worm-wood (?). Woe to those who have not gone forward upon the Way; woe to those who have not passed on by the way-stone! They hated Life's Treasure-House,[4] Miryai, the dear Truth.

"My brothers, hold fast, be a companionship of Miryai. I will look round in the world, let Life's call sound forth and rouse the sleeping and wake [them]."

The eagle flew off from the tree; he wheeled round and instructed his friends. He speaks to them: "Give ear to me, my

---

[1] Presumably the Seven.

[2] Presumably the End-Sea.

[3] White for purity, the M. colour *par excellence*. The water is of course the Living Water or Water of Life.

[4] Or Treasury, Sīmath-Haiyē, a feminine personification, called elsewhere the 'Mother of all the [Light] Kings'; she is *par excellence* the Treasure or Treasury of Light.

brothers! Stay fast and endure persecution. Be a companionship to Miryai. Woe to the Jews, who were a persecution for Miryai! Woe to Elizar, the great house, the pillar that props the temple! Woe to Zatan, the pillar,[1] who has witnessed lies against Miryai!"

THE JEWS PERSECUTE THE MANDÆANS (§ 35 CONTD.).

ALL the Jews gathered together, the teachers, the great and the little; they came [together] and spake of Miryai:

"She ran away from the priests, fell in love with a man, and they took hold of each other's hands. Hold of each other's hands they took, went forth and settled at the mouth of Euphrates. We will slay them and make Miryai scorned in Jerusalem. A stake[2] will we set up for the man who has ruined Miryai and led her away. There shall be no day in the world when a stranger[3] enters Jerusalem."

They split open their fellings and catch the doves in Jerusalem.[4]

THEY BEG THEM TO RETURN (§ 35 CONTD.).

ALL the Jews gathered together and followed after Miryai. They went and found that a throne was set up for Miryai on the bank of Euphrates. A white standard was for her unfurled and a book stood upright on her lap. She reads in the Books of Truth and rouses all worlds from their sleep. She holds in her hand the staff of Life's water; the girdle is bound round her loins. Miryai in humbleness prays and proclaims with wondrous voice. The fishes gather out of the sea, the birds[5] from the mouth of Euphrates. They come to hear Miryai's voice, and no more long to lie down to sleep. They breathe in the sweet scent around her and forget the world.

[1] Mentioned also in § 32, but unexplained.

[2] In the Lud (cp. note on R. Eliezar, founder of the Lud school in §18, p. 34) Ben Stada Talmūd Jesus stories, Jeshu is stoned and hanged on a stake afterwards (see *D. J. L. 100 B.C.?*—pp. 176ff.). It was the custom for the dead body after the stoning (*e.g.* of an adulterer, or of a fornicator—*i.e.* heretic) to be exposed on a stake or post.

[3] Gnosis of Life is called the Stranger (*sc.* to the world) *par excellence*.

[4] The MM. were bitterly persecuted. The fellings or slaughterings of the 'trees' and the snaring or imprisonment of the 'doves' refer to the martyrdom of the faithful. Cp. the hewing-down of the 'trees' in the Synoptic John-sermon and also the John-Jonah (Dove) word-play.

[5] 'Fishes' and 'birds' are the new 'hearers' of the faith.

When the Jews saw this, they stood up before her. They felt shamed, doubled their fists, smote on the fore-court of their breast and lamented. The mother of Miryai spake, and tears streamed into her bosom.

"Look on me, Miryai, my daughter," says she unto her; "look on me who am thy mother! My daughter art thou and the daughter of all of the priests. Thy head is the great chief of the temple. Rememberest thou not, Miryai, that the Torah lay on thy lap? Thou didst open it, read therein and knewest what stands in it. The outer keys lay in thy hands, and the inner thou didst put in chains.[1] All the priests and priests' sons came and kissed thy hand. For whom thou wouldst, thou didst open the door; whom thou wouldst not, must turn and go back to his seat. A thousand stand there and two thousand sit there. They submit themselves to thee, as a eunuch-made slave, and they give ear to thy word in Jerusalem. Why didst thou forget thy brothers and thy heart abandon the priests? Lo, the brides weep in Judæa, the women and men in Jerusalem. Their beloved gold have they cast from them, and they give themselves up to wailing and mourning for thee. They say: 'We will make away with our goods, until Miryai returns. Gold forge we [? no longer], and cast away fair raiments of silk and bracelets (?).' They stand on the roofs and look out, that they may see thee again in Jerusalem. For thee they make vows, if thou comest to me and we go hence. My daughter, arise, come back to thy dwelling-place, the city Jerusalem. Come, light up thy lamps, which have been put out from the day when thou withdrewest thyself.[2] Have no longing after this man, who has prisoned thee and taken thee off. Leave

[1] Presumably kept hidden, or made conditions concerning their revelation.

[2] Compare with the above eloquent invitation to return the similar motive in the Talmūd Jesus stories: (1) "When King Jannai directed the destruction of the Rabbis, R. Joshua ben Perachiah and Jeshu went to Alexandria. When security returned, R. Simeon ben Shetach sent him a letter to this effect: 'From me, Jerusalem the holy city, to thee, Alexandria in Egypt, my sister. My spouse tarries in thee, and I dwell desolate'" (*Bab. Sanhedrim*, 107b, *Sota*, 47a). (2) "The inhabitants of Jerusalem intended to appoint Jehuda ben Tabbai as Nasi [Prince or President of the Sanhedrim] in Jerusalem. He fled and went away to Alexandria, and the inhabitants of Jerusalem wrote: 'From Jerusalem the Great to Alexandria the Little: How long lives my betrothed with thee, whilst I am sitting grieving for him?'" (*Pal. Chagiga*, 77d). See my *D. J. L 100 B.C.?*—pp. 137ff., 148ff.—for a discussion of these passages. Can Tabbai possibly in any way connect with the Tab-Yōmīn of the Portents-piece § 18?

the man, who is not of thy dwelling-place,¹ alone by himself in the world. Let him not say: I have gone and carried off Miryai from her place. Come, teach the children, so that they may learn. Lay the Torah in thy lap and let us hear thy voice as it used to be. From the moment and the day when thou didst detach the dough² has it been covered up . . . ."

When Miryai heard this from her mother, she laughed and rejoiced in her mind. "It *surely* could not be the Jews," says she unto her, "the infamous, worthless priests! It surely would not be the Jews who stand there and bow down to a brick-grave!³ They shall be buried in the Darkness.

"Go, go," says she unto them, "ye fools, ye abortions,⁴ ye who were not of the world.⁵ I am no woman who is stripped for wantoning; and it is not that I have fallen in love with a man. Stripped am I not for returning to you and for again seeing you, doming of blasphemy. Go, go hence from me, ye who have witnessed falsehood and lying against me. Against me ye wit-

¹ Clearly indicating that the Mandā was originally not Jewish.

² Heb. *ḥallah*, the priests' share of the dough. Cp. Lev. xv. 20, 21: "Of the first of your dough (marg. coarse meal) ye shall offer up a cake for a heave-offering."

³ Cp. L.'s note (p. 114¹), referring to the above-quoted (p. 68, n. 2) Talmūd passage (1), where the same bowing down is recorded of Jeshu, namely: "he set up a brick-bat and worshipped it." L. again prefers to render the two words here as 'vault' simply. The Talmūd puzzle has never been solved; but the passage of the J. B. above (p. 55) connects it with a coffin, and strongly suggests an Egyptian atmosphere. Cp. now what Josephus (*Antiqq.* I. ii.; Cory's *An. Fragg.* pp. 171, 172), Hebraïzing the Egyptian tradition, says of the Sons of Sēth (=Sōthis=Sirius), how "they made two [kinds of] monuments, one of brick and the other of stone, and on each engraved their discoveries." This passage is from Manetho's lost work *Sothis*, on the authenticity of which and its implications, I would refer the reader to my lengthy researches in *Thrice-greatest Hermes*, i. 99-127: the above passage will be found on p. 114. From this I would venture to suggest that the Talmūd charge against Jeshu of learning 'magic' in Egypt is reflected in the queer term 'brick-bat' or 'bricking.' According to Manetho's legend or tradition the most ancient lore of the priests, of the period of the First Thoth or Hermes, before the Flood, was preserved in the most primitive brick pyramids. The pyramids were originally tombs. That my suggested version is in the right direction is borne out by the following sentence of the text: "They shall be *buried* in the Darkness."

⁴ A common Gnostic figure, appearing frequently in Manichæism. In the Christianized Gnosis it is the technical term for the unripe birth from Achamōth, the Wisdom Without. For the most interesting echo in the N.T. cp. Paul's famous utterance: "And last of all he appeared unto me also, as unto 'the Abortion'"—*sc.* of whom you have all heard.

⁵ This is presumably ironical = "who thought that ye were not of this world."

nessed wantonness and thieving, and held me up as ye are yourselves. Blessed be the Man who freed me from my fetters and planted my feet here. No wantonness have I committed with him and attempted no theft in the world. Instead of the witness ye have witnessed against me, there came to me prayer and praise-giving."

As the priests stand there and speak with Miryai at the mouth of Euphrates, there came a pure eagle-bird, whose wings are the fulness of worlds.[1] He flew down on the Jews, dashed at them with his wings, bound them and sank them down unto the water's bottom, deeper [down] than the foul-smelling mud. He sank them deeper down than the blazing [water], that is inside the dark water. He sank their ships down to the blazing water's bottom. He destroyed the temple and laid fire to Jerusalem.[2]

He brought downfall upon them and in Jerusalem slew the disciples.

He descended unto her (Miryai), folded before her his wings, settled down by her, narrated and proclaimed to her; and they held out the loved hand of Truth to each other. He embraced her in potent embracing, forced her down and set her on the throne.

"Miryai," he speaks to her, "with favour look upon me, remember me in the Life's presence. I am thy Good Messenger, the Man, who gives ear to thy discourse. I beseech thee for the high Truth, the Truth which the Jordans have chosen."

"O Good Treasure," she makes answer unto him, "Treasure whom Life has sent! Thy glory and thy light has risen upon us, and thy honour is approved in Light's region. Everyone who gives ear to thy voice, will be in the pure region included. In Life's Treasury will he be included and thy rays will rise [over him] twofold. For everyone who gives not ear to thy voice, waking and sleep will be wiped out. Let him belong to the Jews, to the slaves and all of the priests, the sons of the Harlot. I and thou will circle aloft and victorious mount to Light's region."

May Life be our pledge, and Life is victorious.

---

[1] That is, presumably, fill the whole of the worlds in their span.

[2] The MM. evidently believed that the destruction of Jerusalem was a retribution for the persecution of their community.

III.—SOME TYPICAL EXTRACTS.

UNDER the first two headings readers have been made acquainted with all those pieces from the Mandæan John-Book that can be held to have in any sense a historic intention. To these are now added a few extracts of such specimens of the rest of the contents as do not require a commentary.

We will begin with 'The Fisher of Souls' tractate from the John-Book. It seems to me to throw great light on the symbolic phrase of the gospels, indeed to give it a background, and not to be explained in reverse order as the Mandæan expansion of an isolated Christian expression.

THE FISHER OF SOULS SAGA (§§ 36-39)[1].

In the Name of Great Life may hallowed Light be glorified.

A FISHER am I, a Fisher who elect is among fishers. A Fisher am I who among the fishers is chosen, the Head of all catchers of fish. I know the shallows of the waters, the inner . . . and the . . . 1 fathom; I come to the net-grounds, to the shallows and all fishing-spots, and search the marsh in the dark all over. My boat is not cut off [from the others] and I shall not be stopped in the night.

I see the fish[2] in (? on) the dike. I pressed forward on the way with a . . . that was not of iron. I covered (?) the . . . which was for us an obstruction. Aside did I push the swimmers

---

[1] This section is the most difficult of all to translate owing to the abundance of technical fishing terms. In spite of marvellous philological industry and wide-flung enquiries L. has been unable to identify a number of words.

[2] *Sc.* the faithful.

F

who hinder Life's way. On my head I set up a . . . in whose shadow the fish sit. The fisher-trident which I have in my hand, is instead a *margnā* select, a staff of pure water, at whose sight tremble the fishers.

I sit in a boat of glory and come into this world (Tibil) of the fleeting. I come to the water's surface; thither to the surface of the water I drew, and I drew to the crossing's surface. I come in a . . . , in slow, steady course. The water by my boat is not ruffled, and no sound of my boat is heard. Before me stands Hibil (Abel), at my side Shitil (Seth) of sweet name is to be seen, close by me, close in front of me, Anōsh (Enoch) sits and proclaims.

They say: "O Father, Good Fisher, hallo! O Fisher of loveable name!"

Close by me, close near my boat, I hear the uproar (?) of the fishers, the fishers who eat fish,[1] and their stench rushes on me,— the uproar of the fishers and the uproar of their mongers who revile and curse one another. Everyone accuses the other. The buyer says to the fisher: "[Take back?] thy fish! They are stinking already, and no one wants to buy them off of me. Thou makest the catch far out at sea,[2] so that loss falls on the buyer."

Thereon speaks the fisher and makes the man, his customer, hear: "A curse on thee, a curse on thy buyers, a curse on thy bell,[3] a curse on thy boat for not filling up. Thou hast brought no salt and sprinkled it over thy fish which thou boughtest, so that the fish of thy boat will not be stinking and thou then canst sell for hard cash. Next, hast thou no meal and no dates brought, no salt . . . hast thou brought. If then thou comest with empty hands, one who is of fair favour has no dealing with thee. Go, go, thou godless [fellow], buy not from us to do business with thy fraudulent scales. Thou holdest them down to buy at false weight, [then in selling] keepest them up with thy elbow and gettest ten for five. Now does thy buying flee away, and thy buyer, and is as though it never had been. Thou dost complain of the . . . of men and dost cherish no noble thought."

[1] *Sc.* the Seven.

[2] Lit. 'on the high sea.' L. glosses this as meaning that they are not river fish; but this seems to me unnecessary, as my rendering suggests.

[3] Used apparently by the fish-seller for advertising his wares.

When the Chief Fisher, the Head of the race of the Living, the highest of all catchers of fish, heard this, he said to him (? Anōsh): "Bring me my . . . , hand me the *squbrā*,[1] that I may make a call sound forth into the marsh, that I may warn the fish of the depths and scare away the foul-smelling birds that pursue after my fish. I will catch the great *sidmā*,[2] and tear off his wings on the spot. I will take from him * * * and will blow into my *squbrā*. A true *squbrā* is it, so that the water may not mix with pitch."

When the fishers heard the call, their heart fell down from its stay. One calls to the other and speaks to him: "Go into thy inner ground. For there is the call of the Fisher, the Fisher who eats no fish. His voice is not like that of a fisher, his *squbrā* not like our *squbrā*. His voice is not like our voice, his discourse not like to this world."

But the fishers stand there; they seek not shelter in their inner ground. As the fishers stand there and are thinking it over, the Fisher came swiftly upon them; he opened the cast-net, divided . . . . He cast them bound into the . . . . He tied them up with knots. They speak to him: "Free us from our bonds, so that thy fish may not leap up to our boat. We catch not those who name thy Name."

When the fishers thus spake to me, I smote them with a club made of iron. I bound their traders on the shore which lends not . . . (?). I roped them with ropes of bast and broke up their ships * * * *. I burnt up the whole of their netting and the . . . which holds the nets together. I threw chains round them and hung them up aft on my ship's stern. I made them take an oath, took from them their mystery, in order that they may not catch the good fish,—that they may not steal them from me, stick them on a cane, hang them up,[3] cut them in pieces and throw them into baskets (?) with laurel and aloe. They (the fishers) are laid low and cannot rise up. The nets . . . ., and they no longer stab the fisher-trident into the Jordan. They do not cut off * * * * * * and stand not in the river-lands

---

[1] Evidently a wind-instrument of some kind.

[2] Presumably a water-bird.

Sc. to dry in the sun.

and make not their catch in the shallows. They cast not the cast-net therein and take not . . . and aloe.

I spake to those who eat the . . . of the fish whose name is eel. They eat the eel and the . . ., which stands upright on its forefeet. They eat the . . . . I bound them in the marshes of Deception, and they were caught and were tied up. Water from the Ulai they drink not and know not the way to the Kshash river.[1] I bound them fast in their ships, and threw out my ropes to the good ones. To them I speak: "Draw your boat up here, so that it runs not into the dike."

As the Chief of the fish-catchers thus spake, the fishers made answer unto him and said; "Blessed be thou, O Fisher, and blessed be thy boat and thy bark. How fair is thy cast-net, how fair the yarn that is in it. Fair is thy cord and thy lacing, thou who art not like the fishers of this world. On thy meshes are no shell-fish, and thy trident catches no fish. Whence art thou come hither? Tell us! We will be thy hired servants. We will bake and stir about broth and bring it before thee. Eat, and the crumbs which fall from thy hand,—these will we eat and therewith be filled."

But I made answer unto them: "O ye fishers, who lap up your filth, no fisher am I who fishes for fish, and I was not formed for an eater of filth. A Fisher am I of souls who bear witness to Life. A Poor Fisher am I who calls to the souls, collects them together and gives them instruction. He calls to them and bids them come and gather together unto him. He says unto them: If ye . . . come, ye shall be saved from the foul-smelling birds I will save my friends, bring them on high and in my ship make them stand upright. I will clothe them with vestures of glory and with precious light will enwrap them. I will put a crown of æther upon them and what else for them the Greatness erects on their head. Then sit they on thrones and in precious light do they glisten. I bear them thither and raise them aloft; but ye Seven shall stay here behind. The portion of filth and of filthy

---

[1] K. is the infernal river which the souls have to cross after death; its waters are figured as dragons and its waves as scorpions (§ 51). Ulai is also a river. If it is in any way connected with the Eulæus from which the Kings of Persia are fabled to have drunk, the sense is hard to find. It is more probably an infernal stream, at any rate one from which the evil fishers drank.

doings shall be your portion. On the day when the Light ascends, the Darkness will return to its region. I and my disciples will ascend and behold the Light's region."

Life is exalted and is victorious, and victorious is the Man who has come hither.

THE LIGHT-SHIP OF THE FISHER (§ 37).

In the Name of Great Life may hallowed Light be glorified.

A FISHER am I of Great Life, a Fisher am I of the Mighty; a Fisher am I of Great Life, an Envoy whom Life has sent. It (Life) spake unto me: "Go, catch fish who do not eat filth, fish who do not eat water-fennel and reek not of foul-smelling fennel. They do not come nigh to devour bad dates and get caught in the nets of the marsh."

Life knotted for me a noose and built for me a ship that fades not,—a ship whose wings are of glory, that sails along as in flight, and from it the wings will not be torn off. 'Tis a well-furnished ship and sails on in the heart of the heaven. Its ropes are ropes of glory and a rudder of Truth is there to it. Sunday takes hold of the pole, Life's Son seized the rudder. They draw thither to the shekīnahs and dispense Light among the treasures. Thrones in them (*sc.* the shekīnahs) they set up, and long drawn out come the Jordans upon them. On the bow are set lamps that in the wildest of tempests are not put out. All ships that sight me, make obeisance submissively to me. Submissively they make me obeisance and come to show their devotion unto me.

In the bows stands the Fisher and delivers wondrous discourses. [There are] lamps [there], whose wicks shift not hither and thither, and a . . . is not by him. He wears no ring of Deception, and with white robes is he clad. He calls to the fish of the sea and speaks to them: "Give heed to yourselves in the world! Beware of the foul-smelling birds who are above you. If you give heed to yourselves, my brothers, I will for you be a succour,—a succour and a support out of the regions of Darkness unto Light's region."

Life is exalted and is victorious, and victorious is the Man who has come hither.

THE GOOD FISHER REJECTS THE OVERTURES OF THE EVIL ONES AND OVERWHELMS THEM (§ 38).

In the Name of Great Life may hallowed Light be glorified.

THE Fisher clad him with vestures of glory, and an axe hung from his shoulder . . . . . . and commotion of mischief, and a bell is not on the handle.[1] When the fishers caught sight of the Fisher, they came and gathered around him. "Thou art," say they unto him, "a . . . Fisher, thou who hast caught no fish of the marsh. Thou hast not seen the . . . . . . in which the fish gather . . . . We will make thee familiar with the fishers; be our great partner and take a share as we [do]. Grant us a share in thy ship, and take thou a share in our ship. A bargain! Take from us as partner and grant us a share in thy ship. Grant us a share and we will give thee a share in what we possess. Join thy ship with ours and clothe thee in black as we [do], so that, if thou holdest thy lantern on high, thou mayst find something, that the fish may not see thy glory and thy ship may take in fish. If thou dost give ear (to us), thou shalt catch fish, throw them into thy ship and do business. If thou givest no ear to our discourse, thou shalt eat salt; but if thou doest our works, thou shalt eat oil and honey. Thou stirrest a broth, thou fillest a bowl and sharest it with all of the fishers. We appoint thee as head over all of us. The fishers gather together beside thee, the first follow behind thee; they will be thy slaves, and thou takest three shares of what falls to our share. Our father shall be thy servant and we will call ourselves thy bondsmen. Our mother shall sit on thy couch (?)

---

[1] Uncertain. Père Anastase of Baghdad informs L. that now-a-days a bell is attached to the rudder-bar; but here it seems to have some connection with the axe.

and net nets, she shall be thy maid-servant and knit for thee yarns of all kinds. She shall space out the floats of cedar and put the lead-sinkers into the meshes,—meshes, meshes which are then more heavy than all of the world. She shall divide the water by means of the yarns, and when the fish run into them they shall be stopped. Then they know not the way that they seek, and have no wit to turn back to their way. Like walls that collapse, they (the nets) come and fall on the good. They do not let the fish rise, nor turn their face to the boulders.[1] They make them sink deep under the mud and shut them into . . . . They collect them into heaps and shake them (?) out of the . . . . There is there a . . . . . . , into which the fish dash and are stopped. On the . . . of the . . . wattle-work is set up between two machines. Nets are laid down and . . . ., which are filled with bad dates as bait, which cause them to eat death. Woe to the fish who is blinded by them, whose eye sees not the Light. Wise are the fish who know them. They pass by all of the baits. [The others] repair thither and . . . , and the nets will be for them there a lodging. One of a thousand sees it and of two thousand two see it. Its . . . is closed, and a bell is hung on its side-door,—a bell that is forged in mischief and catches the whole of the world. There, is the water mingled with fennel . . . . the pegs (?) of death. Woe to the fish who fall into them."[2]

When the Fisher heard this, he stamped on the bows of the ship. The Fisher stamped on the ships of the fishers; the fishers lie in the shallows close crowded together, tied up together like bundles of wheat, and cannot rise up. The reeds swish . . .,[3] and the fish of the sea lie over the fishers. They snarl in the marsh and the water rings them round in its circle (?).

Then shrilling he spake with his voice. He discoursed with his voice sublime and spake to the catchers of fish: "Off from me,

[1] L. suggests so as to seek the spawning places or in order to hide themselves.

[2] The numerous gaps which have to be left owing to uncertainty of translation make a number of the above sentences unintelligible. The concluding paragraphs are presumably an allegory of the attractions of false religions, and can hardly be thought to be part of the speech of the fishers.

Presumably as the waves made by the foundering ships reach the shore.

ye foul-smelling fishers, ye fishers who mix poison. Begone, begone, catch fish, who [eat?] your own filth. Down with you to your . . . and go to the end of the crossing. I am no Fisher who catches fish, and my fish are tested. They are not caught by the hook with bad dates, a mess which [my?] fish do not eat. They fall not into the nets that are coloured[1] and turn not to the lamps of the Lie. They sink not down through the mud of the water, and go not after the . . . of Deception. They (? the nets) divide not the water * * * * * *, that shall fall on the good. If the fishers cast o'er them the cast-net, they tear asunder the net and set themselves free. There will be no day in this world on which the fishers catch [my?] fish. There will be no day in this world on which the dove loves the ravens. Accursèd be ye, ye foul-smelling birds, and accursèd your nest, so that it may not be filled. Woe to your father Sirmā,[2] whose bed is in the reeds. Woe to thee, hungry Safnā, whose wings do not dry in this world.[3] Woe to thee, foul-smelling Sagiā, thou who seest the fish and sighest [for them]. He shrieks and cries bitterly, when he strikes for the fish and misses them. Woe to thee, Arbānā . . ., thou who haulest the fish out of the deeps. Well for him who frees himself from the talons of those who catch fish. Well for him who frees himself from the men who are watchers of this world. Begone, begone with you, ye Planets, be of your own houses a portion. Water does not mix with pitch, and the Light is not reckoned as Darkness. The perfect ones' partner cannot be called your partner. The good (sing.) cannot belong to the wicked (pl.) nor the bad to the good. Your ship cannot be tied up with mine, nor your ring (?) be laid on my ring. There, is the head of all of you; count yourselves unto *his* realm! This your crass father stays stuck in the black water. Your mother, who nets nets and heavy double machines, have I beaten with the staff of (living) water and smashed a hole in her head. I lead on my friends, raise them on high in my ship and guide them past all the tax-gatherers.[4] I guide them through the passage of outrage,

---

[1] The Mandæan colour is white.

[2] In the M. text, 146, 12, this is given as Sidmā. L. thinks it is a water-fowl of some kind.

Presumably because it is always diving after its prey.

[4] Sc. the Seven.

the region where the fishes are taken. I make them escape the fish-eaters. But ye will come to an end in your dwellings. I and my friends of the Truth will find a place in Life's shekīnah. Into the height will I bear them on thrones surrounded with standards of glory.

The Seven are vanquished and the Stranger-Man stays victorious. The Man of piety put to the test was victorious and helped the whole of his race unto victory.

Life is exalted and is victorious, and victorious is the Man who has come hither.

THE FINAL SUBMISSION OF THE EVIL FISHERS (§ 39).

In the Name of Great Life may hallowed Light be glorified.

'TIS the voice of the Pure Fisher who calls and instructs the fish of the sea in the shallows. He speaks to them: "Raise your ... up, on the surface of the water stand upright; then will your force be double as great. Guard yourselves from the fishers who catch the fish and beat on the Jordan.[1] Shilmai and Nidbai[2] curse them, and they depart and settle themselves down behind me a mile off. The fish curse their casting-net ... ... in their place."

When the Fisher thus spake, warning all [of the fish, when] the fishers his voice heard, they came up and gathered around him. They put themselves forward to ask of him questions, and knew not whence he came. "Where wast thou, Fisher," they ask him, "that we heard not thy voice in the marsh? Thy ship is not like our ship, and thy ... is not * * * * * *. Thy ship is not tarred over with pitch, and thou art not like the fishers of this world."

The fishers see him, become scarlet for shame and remain standing in their places. They say to him: "Whence comes it

---

[1] *Sc.* to frighten the fish into the nets.
[2] The Jordan-Watchers.

that thou dost fish without finding? Thy ship is not like our ship; it shines by night' like the sun. Thy ship is perfected in æther, and wondrous standards are unfurled above it. Our ship sails along in the water, but thy ship between the waters. Our reeds (? rods) grumble at one another and break into pieces. Among them is the fish-trident of wrath, on which ... and ...... are not. Thy ......, O Fisher, is such that when the fish see it, they take themselves off. We have not yet seen any fishers which are like unto thee. The wind wafts thy ship on, the mast ...... for the fisher and a rudder that gleams in the water-shallows. On thy cast-net is no cord, and they have not laid ...... ¹ round it. There are no ... ... in it, which are a cunning device against the fish of the .... Thou keepest thy yarn ...... and hast no clapper and no hatchet. Thy yarn (= net) fishes not in the water and is not coloured for catching fish."

When the fishers thus spake, the Fisher made answer unto them: "Have done, ye fishers and fishers' sons; off, get you gone from me! Off, go up to your village, the Ruins, Jerusalem. Ask about me of your father, who knows me, ask of your mother, who is my maid-servant. Say to him: There is a Fisher in the boat, in which are four .... [There is] a rudder, and it stands there, and a mast ....² and redemptions. They lay waste the land of Jerusalem."

When they heard this from the Fisher who has come hither, and understood, they spake to him: "Have compassion, forbearance and mercy on us and forgive us our sins and transgressions. We are thy slaves, show thyself indulgent towards us. We will look after thy fish that none of them fails. We will be the servants of thy disciples, who name thy Name in Truth. We will continue to look after all who name thy Name."

Life is exalted and is victorious, and victorious is the Man who has come hither.

Other pieces set forth such figures as those of 'The

¹ Bait of some kind presumably.

² Detailing probably the remaining two of the four objects referred to.

Heavenly Plough' and of 'The Sowers'; but perhaps the most interesting is the saga of 'The Good Shepherd.' Here again it is difficult to believe that it was derived from Christian sources; it seems to be as independent as the Fisher of Souls' figure. The 'discourse' runs as follows:

THE GOOD SHEPHERD (§ 11).

In the Name of Great Life may hallowed Light be glorified.

A SHEPHERD am I who loves his sheep; sheep and lambs I watch over. Round my neck [I carry] the sheep; and the sheep from the hamlet stray not. I carry them not to the sea-shore, that they see not the whirl of the water, may not be afraid of the water, and if they are thirsty may not drink of the water.[1] I bear them away [from the sea], and water them with the cup of my hand, until they have drunken their fill. I bring them unto the good fold; and they feed by my side. From the mouth of Euphrates, from the mouth of Euphrates the Radiant,[2] things of marvellous goodness I brought them. I brought them myrtle, white sesame brought them and brought them bright standards.[3] I cleansed them and washed them and made them to smell the sweet odour of Life. I put round them a girdle, at sight of which the wolves tremble. No wolf leaps into our fold; and of no fierce lion need they be alarmed. Of the tempest they need not be frightened; and no thief can break in upon us. A thief breaks not into their fold; and of a knife[4] they need not be anxious.

When my sheep were quietly laid down and my head lay there on the threshold, a rift was rent in the height and thunder did thunder behind me. The clouds seized hold one of another,

---

[1] The salt, bitter, water of the sea of death and destruction, as opposed to the fresh, sweet water, the living water or water of Life.

[2] Equating with the Heavenly Jordan.

[3] All symbolic objects in the cult.

Sc. the knife or sword of the Angel of Death.

and unchained were the raging tempests. Rain poured down in sheets and hail that smites elephants low, hail that shatters the mountains. And the tempests unchain themselves in an hour.[1] Seas burst forth; they flooded the whole of the world. There, under the water, no one escaped, once he sank from the height as into a gulf. The water swept off everyone who had no wings or no feet.[2] He speeds on, and knows not he speeds; he goes, and knows not he goes. Thereupon I sprang up and I entered the fold to bear my sheep forth from their place. I saw my eyes full.[3] I saw the sea, I saw the fierce-raging tempest, I saw the storm-clouds that send forth no [friendly] greeting the one to the other. Ten-thousand times ten-thousand dragons are in each single cloud. I weep for my sheep, and my sheep weep for themselves. The little lambs are lamenting who cannot come out of the fold's door.

When then * * * * * *, I entered the house,[4] I mounted up to the highest place [in it], and I call to my sheep. To the sheep in my care do I call. I pipe to them; I get them to hear, so that they come unto me. To them I pipe on my pipe, and beat on my tabour (?), [leading them] to the water.[5] I call to them: "My little sheep, little sheep, come! Rise up at my call! Come, rise at my call; then will you 'scape the cloud-dragons. Come, come unto me! I am a shepherd whose boat is soon coming. My boat of glory is coming; and I come with it, and bring my sheep and lambs in aboard it. Every one who gives ear to my call and heed gives unto my voice, and who turns his gaze unto me, of him take I hold with my hands and bring him unto me inboard my boat." But every lamb, male and female, that suffered himself to be caught, the water-whirl carried away, the greedy water did swallow. Whoever gave no ear to my call, sank under. To the highest part of the vessel I went. The bows stand up with the bow-post.[6] I say: How woeful am I for my sheep who

---

[1] This may mean at a certain period or appointed time.

[2] The faithful are figured as birds as well as sheep.

[3] An untranslatable idiom.

[4] *Sc.* of this world.

That is, the living water.

This is conjectural.

because of the mud have sunk under. The water-whirl sank them away from my reach, the swirling whirl of the water. How grieved am I for the rams whose fleece on their sides has dragged them down into the deep. How grieved am I for the lambkins whose bellies have not [yet] been filled full of milk. Of a thousand, one I recovered; of a whole generation I found again two. Happy is he who [stood up?] in the water, and in whose ears no water has entered. Happy the great rams who have stamped with their feet. Happy is he who has escaped from the Seven and Twelve, the sheep-stealers. Happy is he who has not couched down, has not lain down, has not loved to sleep deeply. Happy is he who in this defective age of Bishlom[1] has stayed whole. Happy are they who free themselves from the snares of Rūhā (the Mother World-Spirit), from the filth and the shame and the bondage that have no end. My chosen! whoever shall live at the end of this age of Nirig (Mars), for him let his own conscience be a support. He will come and mount up to the Radiant Dwelling, to the region whose sun never sets, and whose light-lamps[2] never darken.

Life is exalted and is victorious, and victorious is the Man who has come hither.

THE LOVING SHEPHERDS OF THE GOOD SHEPHERD (§ 12).

In the Name of Great Life may hallowed Light be glorified.

A TREASURE calls from without hither and speaks.

"Come, be for me a loving shepherd and watch me a thousand out of ten thousand."—

"So then will I be a loving shepherd for thee and watch thee a thousand out of ten thousand. But how full is the world of vileness and sown full of thorns and of thistles!"—

"Come, be for me a loving shepherd and watch me a thousand

---

[1] Lidzbarski (p. 465) thinks this refers to the Moslim period. Elsewhere we find the parallel phrase 'age of Bizbat,' which L. also refers to Muḥammad. But Bizbat is clearly a corrupt form of Baal-Zebul, and therefore the reference should be more general.

[2] Presumably stars.

out of ten thousand. I will bring thee then sandals of glory with them canst thou tread down the thorns and the thistles. Earth and heaven decay, but the sandals of glory decay not. Sun and moon decay, but the sandals of glory decay not. The stars and heaven's zodiacal circle decay, but the sandals of glory decay not. The four winds of the [world-] house decay, but the sandals of glory decay not. Fruits and grapes and trees decay, but the sandals of glory decay not. All that is made and engendered decays, but the sandals of glory decay not. So then be for me a loving shepherd and watch me a thousand out of ten thousand."—

"I will then be a loving shepherd for thee and watch thee a thousand out of ten thousand. But if a lion comes and carries off one, how am I to retrieve him? If a thief come and steals one away, how am I to retrieve him? If one falls into the fire and is burnt, how am I to retrieve him? If one falls into the water and drowns, how am I to retrieve him? If one stays behind in the pen, how am I to retrieve him?"—

"Natheless, come therefore, be for me a loving shepherd and watch me a thousand out of ten thousand. If a lion comes and carries off one, let him go his way and fall a prey to the lion. Let him go his way and fall a prey to the lion, in that he bows himself down to the sun. If a wolf comes and carries off one let him go his way and fall a prey to the wolf, in that he bows himself down to the moon. If a thief comes and steals away one, then let him go his way and fall a prey to the thief. Let him go his way and fall a prey to the thief, in that he bows himself down before Nirig (Mars). If one falls into the fire and is burnt, let him go his way and fall a prey to the fire. Let him go his way and fall a prey to the fire, in that he bows himself down to the fire. If one falls into the mud and stays stuck there, then let him go his way and fall a prey to the mud. Let him go his way and fall a prey to the mud, in that he bows himself down to Messiah. If one falls into the water and drowns, then let him go his way and fall a prey to the sea. Let him go his way and fall a prey to the sea, in that he bows himself down to the seas. If one stays behind in the pen, let him go his way and fall a prey to the pen-demon.[1] Let him go

---

[1] Spirit or jinn (?)

his way and fall a prey to the pen-demon, in that he bows himself down to the idols. . . . . . .[1] Come, be for me a loving shepherd and watch me a thousand out of ten thousand."[2]—

"So will I then be for thee a loving shepherd and watch thee a thousand out of ten thousand. I will watch a thousand of thousands, yea of ten thousand those who adore him."[3]

"But some of them wander from me. I went up into high mountains and went down into deep valleys. I went and found him where he can crop nothing. Of each single sheep I took hold with my right hand and on the scale did I lay him. A thousand among ten thousand have the [right] weight."

Life is exalted and is victorious, and victorious is the Man who has come hither.

The next piece I have selected, treats of the source of all glory and enlightenment, called the Treasury of Life, that in which all spiritual powers and blessings are stored. The origin of the motive is without doubt the Iranian concept of the *hvareno*, the divine and kingly glory. In the Mandæan tradition it has become highly developed and is frequently personified as a female greatness. Thus in the Oxford MS. F. it is spoken of as "the Mother of all the Kings [of the Light], from whom all worlds have come forth, who separated herself from the fervency of the Hidden Mysteries." Many *rôles* are assigned to this Light of Life in the complexities of the celestial and cosmic dramas; and in the human stage it shines forth as the glory with which the perfected are vestured and

[1] A still more degraded form of cult is mentioned, but the meaning baffles the translator; it is referred to those who bow down before Rūhā, here in mockery called 'Holy' Spirit.

[2] The above is obscure, especially the 'pen-demon' reference. The general sense, however, seems to be that those who fall away from the Mandæan faith are not to be restrained by force, but let go their way.

[3] *Sc.* Life. The concluding paragraph runs on without break in the German, being assigned to the same speaker; but the subject is clearly changed and the whole spirit is different. The Good Shepherd now seeks for the lost sheep and does not leave it to perish.

crowned. I have chosen the simplest of the narratives or discourses on the topic. In the still more complex system of the phase of development represented by the *Pistis Sophia* collection there is no mention of the Treasury of Life, but the Treasury of Light is one of its most important conceptions. The Mandæan tradition conserves the echoes of an earlier phase, for it is indubitably less over-worked.

THE TREASURY OF LIFE (§ 57).

In the Name of Great Life may hallowed Light be glorified.

THE Treasury am I, Life's Treasury (Sīmath-Haiyē); the Treasury am I, the Mighty One's Treasury; the Treasury am I, Life's Treasury. A crown was I for the Mighty from everlasting.

The Treasury am I, Life's Treasury. Ever did I give light to the treasures and to the shekīnahs, and was for adornment to Jordan. For adornment became I to Jordan, who was from everlasting, through whom the treasures give light. Great [Life] made me limpid and lucent and made me into a vesture. He made me into his vesture, which day in and day out sings measureless praise of the Æther.

The Treasury am I, Life's Treasury. To the King of the Splendour became I a crown. The treasures shine through my glory and praise my form beyond measure.

The Treasury am I, Life's Treasury—I who as adornment settled down on the King of the Splendour, so that he shone in his mind, that he became bright and shining, and his form glittered more than the [light-] worlds. As I (lit. it) gave light and enlightenment unto the treasures and to the shekīnahs [e'en] in the Æther, the King laid me as vesture round Nᵉṣab the Radiant.[1] Nᵉṣab the Radiant then took me, brought me and laid me as vesture o'er Jordan. As vesture o'er Jordan he laid me, through whom the treasures shine beyond measure.

The Treasury am I, Life's Treasury. The wicked are blind

In § 9 (p. 39) N. is called the Watcher who has his station in every region, *i.e.* the Great Watcher.

and see not. I call them unto the Light, yet they busy themselves with the Darkness. "O ye wicked," I unto them cry, "ye who sink down in the Darkness, arise and fall not into the deep." I cry unto them; yet the wicked hear not and sink into the great Sea of the Ending. Therefore was Jordan made a bridge for the treasures; a bridge for the treasures became he, while he cut off the wicked and hurled them into the great Sea of the Ending.

The Treasury am I, Life's Treasury. A crown I became for Life's Gnosis. He bestowed on me the rulership over the treasures and the shekīnahs which are there [yonder].

The Treasury am I, Life's Treasury. Of the light-worlds was I the enlightener. Day in and day out they sing praise to Great [Life], and through me they mount upward and behold the Light's region.

The Treasury am I, Life's Treasury. A vesture for the light-worlds became I.

[The Treasury] am I, Life's Treasury. A King for the Nazōræans became I. I became a King for the Nazōræans, who through my Name find praise and assurance. Praise and assurance they find through my Name, and on my Name they mount up and behold the Light's region. For the Men of purity put to the test —[for them] their eye became full of Light. Full of Light was their eye, and in their heart Life's Gnosis took seat. Whoever of me, Life's Treasury, makes his investment, loves not gold and silver, loves not gold and possessions, [loves not] food of the body, and envy with him has no place. Envy found with him no place, and he did not forget his night-prayer. He forgot not the discourses and writings, and he forsook not his Lord's word. He forsook not the prayer of his Father, Life's Gnosis; wherefor into the great End-Sea he falls not. He forgot not Sunday, nor did he neglect the Day's evening. He forgot not the way of Great [Life, the way] of wages and alms. He will be rapt away in the night-prayer, he will be rapt away in shining vestures which have come from Great [Life]. Treasures for him fill up what falls short, and what is empty they load for him full. If he bears a pure load, he is counted with the Men of piety put to the test who separate themselves [from the world] in the Name of Yawar.[1] Life's

[1] Y. is the Helper or Saviour. The shekīnah or celestial abode of Yawar, the Chosen, is the Home of the Blessed (*cp.* J.B. 1894).

Treasury rested upon them, to their form it gave light, and for them a way to Great [Life's] House has been established.

I have called with clear voice and directed hereto the disciples: "The vine who bears fruit, doth ascend; who bears none will here be cut off. Whosoever lets himself be enlightened through me and instructed, ascends and beholds the Light's region; whoever does not let himself be enlightened through me and instructed, is cut off and falls into the great End-Sea."

Life is exalted and is victorious, and victorious is the Man who has come hither.

That the Mandæan religion preserves echoes of a wealth of ancient mythical elements found in Iranian, Babylonian and Semitic traditions is evident on all hands. A process of syncretism had presumably gone on for generations before an impulse from within caused the blending to assume a distinctively Mandæan form; and when this emerged, the preservation of the memory of the process had no interest for the faith and fell back into the depths of the subconscious. At anyrate the writers or recorders of the tractates throughout seem honestly persuaded of the complete independence of their tradition from every other form of religion. They are for ever proclaiming the blessings of loyalty to what they claim to be the original, the one and only, revelation of Truth vouchsafed to the world throughout the ages, and declaring that continued spiritual contact with instructors from on high who mediated this divine wisdom, was still possible. They certainly do not give one the idea of being intellectualists consciously at work on a syncretic synthesis of prior material; on the contrary they seem to live and move in a *milieu* of prophetical outpourings and to have been extremely sensitive to psychical impressions. Inspirational discourses and intuitive interpretations of prophetical utterances seem to have been their delight. The following piece may enable the reader to sense somewhat of the peculiar atmosphere of mystical expectancy in which they sought instruction. The topic is one of the chief points of their questioning—the conflict that arose between the Light and the Darkness in the beginnings and how victory is to be achieved. They were not of course absolute Dualists, for always and everywhere victory lies with Life Everlasting, who transcends not only the Darkness but also the Light.

IN THE BEGINNING (§ 13).

In the Name of Great Life may hallowed Light be glorified.

To you I say and declare, ye chosen and perfect, ye who dwell in the world: Become not of the Darkness a portion, but lift up your eyes to Light's region. From the Evil unto the Good separate yourselves out; from the sinful evil of the region of Darkness separate yourselves out. Love and instruct one another, that your sin and [your] guilt be forgiven you. See and hear and get you instructed, that ye may ascend to Light's region victorious.

The good sit there and are in search; and all who are understanding let themselves be instructed. The good speak, take counsel together and say: "Who will come, who tell me, who will set [it] forth for me, who give me instruction? Who will come, who will tell me whether there was *one* King or *two* [in the beginning]?" The good speak and let themselves be instructed.

"*Two* Kings were there, *two* natures were fashioned—a King of this world and a King from outside of the worlds. The King of this age girt on a sword and [put on] a crown of Darkness. A crown of Darkness he put on his head, and took a sword in his right hand. A sword he took in his right hand; he stands there and slaughters his sons, and his sons slaughter each other. The King from outside of the worlds set a crown of Light on his head. A crown of Light he set on his head, and took Truth in his right hand. Truth in his right hand he took, and stands there and instructs his sons. He stands there and instructs his sons, and his sons instruct one another."

"Who will come, who tell me what was before this? When the heaven was not yet outspread and stars were not yet in it figured, when the earth was not yet condensed and into the water no condensation had fallen, when sun and moon came not as yet into this world, how was the soul then?"

"When the soul still sat in the Bowl,[1] she felt neither hunger nor thirst. When the soul still sat in the Bowl, she had no pains and no faults. When the soul still sat in the Bowl, she felt no cold and no heat. When she still sat in the Bowl, the locks on her forehead[2] were incurled, and an æther-crown sat on her head. Her eyes were light-rays (?), and they gazed on the region of the House of Great [Life]. Her mouth was of pure[st] perfection, and sang the praise of the King of Light's region.

"From the day when the Wicked began to think, evil pictured itself forth in him. He fell into great wrath and ventured a fight with the Light. The Envoy was sent to tread down the power of the rebels.

"They[3] brought living water and into the muddy water they poured it. They brought light-giving light and into the gloomful darkness they cast it. They brought the delightsome wind and into the frantic wind cast it. They brought the living fire and into the consuming fire cast it. They brought the soul, the pure mind, and into the vain body cast it.

"Out of fire and of water was the one heaven spread out. Out of fire and of water have they made dense the earth on the anvil.[4] Out of fire and of water fruits, grapes and trees did arise. Out of fire and of water was imaged the corporeal Adam.

"They fashioned the Envoy and to be head of the generations

---

[1] *Kannā*. L. leaves this technical term untranslated; but in note 4 to p. 4 he shows that it frequently means a wine-cup or wine-bowl. I would therefore venture to connect it with the widespread notion of the *kratēr* or mixing-bowl of souls as handed on, for instance, by Plato in the *Timæus*, presumably from Hither Asian sources. One of the treatises of the *Corpus Hermeticum* is called 'The Cup' or 'The Bowl,' or alternatively 'The Monad.' It was not only the source of souls, but also the Mind into which they had to be dowsed for spiritual baptism or regeneration.

[2] Presumably the rays of glory, signifying a state of contemplation.

[3] The supernal powers.

[4] I can find no explanation of this occasionally recurring figure; it indubitably goes back to some ancient myth.

they sent him. With heavenly voice he called hence into the worlds' disquiet. At the call of the Envoy Adam, who lay there,[1] awoke. Adam, who lay there, awoke and went forth to meet the Envoy: 'Come in peace, O Envoy, Life's Messenger, who hast come from the House of my Father. How firmly is planted withal dear, beautiful Life in his region! But how [meanly] for me has a stool been set up and my dark form sits on it lamenting."

"Thereon the Envoy made answer and spake to the corporeal Adam: 'Thy throne has been set up in beauty, O Adam; and 't is thy form sits here lamenting. All[2] were mindful of thee for thy good and fashioned and sent me to thee. I am come and will give thee instruction, O Adam, and free thee from this world. Give ear and hearken and get thee instructed, and mount to Light's region victorious."

Adam gave ear and had faith.—Hail to him who gives ear after thee[3] and has faith! Adam received the Truth.—Hail to him who receives the Truth after thee! Adam looked up full of hope and ascended.—Hail to him who ascends after thee!

Give ear and hearken and let yourselves be instructed, ye perfect, and ascend to Light's region victorious.

And praisèd be Life.

That the moral instruction given to the Mandæans is excellent may be seen in almost any piece; but there are distinctive collections of ethical exhortation of which the following is an example.

EXHORTATIONS (§ 47).

FROM the Light-region have I (Life's Gnosis) come forth, from thee, thou glorious dwelling. With vestures of glory have I been clad and a crown of victory on my head has been set. I came and found the Nazōræans, how they stand on the shore of the Jordan. I set up my throne and sat down, as a father who sits 'midst his sons.

---

[1] In a number of the Gnostic systems of the Early Christian period the body of the first man is said to lie like a log till the light-spark is breathed into him.

[2] *Sc.* the heavenly powers.

[3] Presumably Adam

The Good sits there and teaches his sons all truth, in which is no error.

My sons! See that you commit no adultery; see that you no theft commit. They who commit adultery and who steal, mount not up to Life's house. They mount not up to Life's house and do not behold Light's region.

My sons! See that you practise no magic and afflict not the soul in the body. The magicians and falsificators are hurled into seething pots and fire is their judge.

My sons! See that ye remove not the boundaries, that the boundary-stone you displace not. The eye of those who remove boundaries, looks not on the Light.

My sons! See that you do not abandon the slave to the hands of his master and the slave-girl to the hands of her mistress; abandon not the weak to the strong. [He who acts otherwise] will be fettered in a distant region, in the tax-gatherers' house;[1] his eyes behold only the Darkness and his foot finds no firm ground.

My sons! See that you take not [to wife] a slave-girl who has not been made free, and thereby bring your sons into the house of a master. For if the slave one day sins, then on the day when his master passes judgment upon him, will the sins which the slave commits, fall on the head of his father.

My sons! See that you are not hinters and that your eyes make no suggestions [sc. to women]. For the hinters and wink-givers will be assigned to the guard-stations. To the guard-stations will they be assigned and be judged with stern justice.

My sons! See that you eat not up interest and interest on interest, else in the dark mountain will you receive judgment.

My sons! See that you pay no homage to the idols, the satans and demons, to the worship of idols and to the lusts of this world; for on the godlings and satans will a stern judgment fall, and they who pray to them will not ascend to Life's house and not look on Light's region.

Give heed to what I have charged you, and let no evidence be given of crime and of lying; on evidence of crime and of lying you will be haled to account 'fore the judge. You will be haled to

---

[1] The region of the lower world-rulers.

account 'fore the judge who judges all worlds. He judges each one according to his works and his merit.

My sons! All that is hateful to you, do not to your neighbours; for in the world into which you have come, is a heavy justice and judgment. Heavy justice and judgment is there therein, and every day will minds made secure in it be chosen. For everyone who is laden, mounts upward; but he who is empty is judged here. Woe to the empty, who stands empty there in the house of the collectors of taxes. When he had it in his hand, he gave nothing; there will he search in his pocket and he will find nothing. The wicked and liars will be hurled into the Darkness. They will into the blazing fire cast, into the blazing fire will they cast him into whose ears the call has been made, but he would not give ear. I showed it him unto his eye, but he would not see; I showed it him, but he would not see with his eye.

Life is victorious, and victorious is the Man who has come hither.

The Mandæans possess a rich collection of liturgical songs and hymns which Lidzbarski has translated for the first time in his excellent edition of them (*Mandäische Liturgien*, Berlin, 1920). From these 236 hymns we choose one of the most typical as a specimen, and as perhaps of more than ordinary interest to the general reader who may have puzzled over the unqualified beatitude "Blessed are the poor." It is taken from the Oxford Collection (Bk. I., No. lvi.) and may be entitled:

THE SONG OF THE POOR'S EXALTATION.

In the Name of Great Life may hallowed Light be glorified.

A POOR MAN am I,[1] who comes out of the [celestial] Fruits,
a Stranger to the world, who comes out of the Distance.

[1] Or "One of the Poor am I." Compare the Ebionim or Poor of early Christianity; the Poor (spiritually) are those who have voluntarily renounced this world's goods.

A Poor man am I, to whom Great Life gave ear,
    a Stranger to this world, whom the Light-treasures made world-strange.
They brought me out of the abode of the good ones;
    ah me! in the wicked ones' dwelling they made me to dwell.
Ah me! they made me to dwell in the wicked ones' dwelling,
    which is filled full of nothing but evil.
It is filled full of nothing but evil,
    filled full of the fire which consumes.
I would not and will not
    dwell in the dwelling of naughtness.
With my power and with my enlightening
    I dwelt in the dwelling of naughtness.
With my enlightening and my praise-giving
    I kept myself stranger to this world.
I stood among them
    as a child who has not a father,
As a child who has not a father,
    as a fruit who has not a tender.
I hear the voice of the Seven,
    who whisper in secret and say:
"Whence is this Stranger man,
    whose discourse is not like to our discourse?
I listened not to their discourse;
    then were they full of wicked anger against me.
Life, who gave ear to my call,
    a Messenger sent forth to meet me.
He sent me a gentle Treasure,
    an armoured, well-armoured Man.
With his pure voice he makes proclamation,
    as the Treasures make in the House of Perfection.
He speaks:
"Poor one, from anguish and fear be thou free!
    Say not: I stand here alone.
For thy sake, O Poor,
    this firmament was outspread,
Was this firmament spread out,
    and stars were pictured upon it.
For thy sake, O Poor,
    this firm land came into existence,

Came into existence this firm land,
> the condensing took form, fell into the water.

For thy sake came the sun,
> for thy sake the moon was revealèd.

For thy sake, O Poor, came the Seven,
> and the Twelve are hither descended.

Thou Poor one! On thy right rests glory,
> on thy left rest [light-] lamps.

Hold steadfast in thy security,
> until thy measure has been completed.

When thy measure has been completed,
> I will myself come to thee.

I will bring thee vestures of glory,
> so that the worlds will long for them, desireful.

I will bring thee a pure, excellent head-dress,
> abundant in infinite light.

I will set thee free from the wicked,
> from the sinners will I deliver thee.

I will make thee dwell in thy shekīnah
> free thee into the region unsullied."

I hear the voice of the Seven,
> who whisper in secret and speak:

"Blessed is he who is to the Poor one a father,
> who is unto the Fruit a tender.

Hail to him whom Great Life knows,
> woe to him whom Great Life knows not."

Hail to him whom Great Life knew,
> who has kept himself stranger to this world,

The world of the defect,
> in which the Planets are seated.

They sit on thrones of rebellion
> and drill their works with the scourge.

For gold and for silver are they disquiet,
> and strife they cast into the world.

Disquiet are they and therein cast strife;
> therefore will they go hence and seethe in the fire.

The wicked shall seethe, and their pomp
> shall vanish and come to an end.

But I with my offspring and kindred
> shall ascend and see the Light's region,

The region whose sun never sets,
  and whose light-lamps never darken—
That region, the state [of the Blessed],
  whereto your souls are called and invited.

And so are our good brothers' souls,
  and the souls of our faithful sisters.

Life is exalted and is victorious, and victorious is the
  Man who has come hither.

III.

THE SLAVONIC JOSEPHUS' ACCOUNT OF THE BAPTIST AND JESUS.

IN *The Antiquities* of the Jewish historian Flavius Josephus there are three passages of outstanding importance for Christian readers, seeing that they are the only external witnesses to Christianity from the first century. As such they have been submitted to the closest cross-examination and scrutiny. The general result of the enquiry into the authenticity of their testimony has established for most scholars the judgment, that we have here to deal not with a homogeneous body of evidence, but with three different witnesses, one of which is distinctly good, another as distinctly bad, and a third very probably good. The passage on John the Baptist is well-nigh universally accepted as affording no grounds for reasonable scepticism, and as therefore providing a most valuable external proof that John was a historical character. The account of Jesus, on the other hand, has been called into most serious question by the vast majority of liberal scholars, and by very many conservatives, on numerous grounds, and chiefly because the writer unequivocally affirms that Jesus was the Messiah,—a statement which no Jew could have made. The third is a reference to James, the brother of Jesus 'called' or 'said to be Messiah'—a hesitation which may fairly be ascribed to Josephus himself. Many then who reject the Jesus-passage as indubitably spurious, accept the James-reference as free from reasonable suspicion, and thus obtain a brief but valuable external first-century evidence for earliest Christianity.

Josephus composed his *Antiquities* in Greek, and completed them in 93/94 A.D. They are a general survey of the traditions and history of his people up to the special period of which he had already treated in detail in his first and most famous work, *The Jewish War*. In describing there the events which led up to the outbreak of the revolt, he treats of all the other religious and political movements in Palestine, even the most insignificant, contemporary with the beginnings of Christianity, and yet he says not a single word about the Baptist or Jesus. This is a very striking and puzzling omission. Where precisely we should expect to find such mention, and where far greater opportunities occur for bringing it in than in *The Antiquities*, we are confronted with 'the silence of Josephus.' The *War* was first of all composed in Aramaic and circulated among the Jews of Palestine and Babylonia, doubtless to convince them of the futility of resisting the might of the Roman arms. Of this original edition, however, no trace has so far been discovered. The work known to us is in Greek. It is not a translation so much as a re-composition very carefully prepared on the models of Greek history; and in this Josephus sought the help of Greek stylists. It reads indeed like an original composition; whatever the Aramaic contained, the work as it now stands has been clearly adapted to suit the mentality of the wider public of the Græco-Roman world and the literary circles of the day to whom it was presented.

This Greek edition was composed between 75 and 79 A.D. It is of course not *impossible* to suppose that in the Aramaic there may have been reference to the John- and Jesus- movements. But why then should Josephus have cut them out, when there is an indubitable passage concerning John and a highly probable reference to Jesus in *The Antiquities*? To conjecture a satisfactory answer to this dilemma is exceedingly difficult; it remains an unsolved *crux*. For had there been any such passages in the Aramaic edition of the *War*, surely Christian apologists would have seized upon them and insisted that they should be restored to the Greek text?—unless by chance they contained matter they would not like to see in wider circulation.

That clear light will ever be thrown on this 'silence of Josephus' problem is hardly to be expected. Nevertheless the subject may be said to have recently entered on a new phase: certain hitherto unknown material has been brought forward, which has forced the problem once more into the arena of controversy; and it may very well be that in the future this new material will have always, directly or indirectly, to be taken into consideration whenever the familiar Josephean passages are reviewed or rediscussed.

There is extant in a number of MSS. a Slavonic or Old Russian translation of the *War*. In this version there are no less than eight pieces referring to John the Baptist (3), Jesus (4) and the first Christians (1). These remarkable passages, of which the Greek text shows no trace, have been excerpted and the Slavonic text of them critically established by the collation of four MSS.

In the first place it is agreed on all hands by the German scholars who have investigated them, that these pieces were not originally composed in Slavonic and interpolated into the translation. Not only is the style foreign to correct Slavonic idiom, but the peculiar nature of the contents is so alien to Slavonic mentality, that to suppose so late a writer as a Slavonic translator, who could at the very earliest be assigned only to the 10th century, is out of the question. They are indubitably translations, and moreover clearly rendered from Greek. This is shown not only by the construction of the sentences in general, but also by the clumsiness and uncertainty of the translator in his rendering of particles and conjunctions; moreover the Greek original for the veil or curtain of the temple (*katapetasma*) is retained.

These eight pieces were excerpted from the rest of the text and first made accessible for the general world of scholarship, in German translation, by A. Berendts, in 1906.[1]

The consensus of learned opinion in Germany (and elsewhere apparently no notice whatever has been taken of the 'find') from the start has been entirely unfavourable to their authenticity. That is to say, no one has so far ventured to claim them for Josephus himself. They were immediately and almost unanimously dismissed as transparent Christian forgeries, and that too of a late date and of no sort of historic value of any kind. Here and there, however, were signs of some hesitation in endorsing so wholesale and precise a verdict; for a few, the matter seemed not so simple as it appeared at first sight. The first *caveat* was entered and the subject brought into a new perspective by R. Seeberg in a somewhat popular but

---

[1] '*Die Zeugnisse vom Christentum im slavischen "De bello judaico" des Josephus*'—*Texte und Untersuchungen*, N.F. xiv. 4.

highly suggestive treatment, which he boldly entitled 'A New Source for the Earliest History of Christianity.'[1] Though Seeberg's reputation as a specialist on questions of origins forbade the rejection of his view as that of an irresponsible eccentric, no attention was paid to it, perhaps because he had not attempted to work out his theory in detail. This task, however, was speedily undertaken by Johannes Frey, of the University of Dorpat, who had just published a very valuable and thorough-going study of the History of the Passion. In 1908 Frey produced a substantial volume,[2] in which he treated the material to an acute analysis and with minute elaboration, and in other respects showed a remarkable grasp of all the puzzling complexities of a whole series of problems which an intensive scrutiny of the passages brought out.

In the first place Frey called attention to the fact that the general characteristics of these pieces were very different from those of all other ancient Christian forgeries known to us. His main contention throughout this very thorough enquiry is that the author, whoever he may have been precisely, must be held in general to be a Jew and not a Christian. There is no evidence of direct dependence on early canonical Christian literature, no sign that he had any acquaintance with the precision of written tradition. In so far as there is agreement with the Gospels or Acts, it is only in respect to the barest generalities; there is nothing even to show acquaintance with the precise inner oral traditions of the Christians themselves. It is all set forth from an external standpoint. Neverthe-

[1] '*Eine neue Quelle zur Geschichte des Urchristentums*,' in the periodical *Reformation*, 1906, NNr. 19 and 20.

[2] *Der slavische Josephusbericht über die urchristliche Geschichte nebst seinen Parallelen*, Dorpat, 1908.

less the writer is not simply fabricating freely out of his imagination. He has traditional material of some sort to go on. He is trying to set forth what he has heard and gathered, and what at times puzzles him considerably. He reports opinion—what people say; some this, others that. He would also play the part of the impartial historian, considering probabilities and even possibilities. He is not a hostile critic by any means; on the contrary, he is in general sympathetic. Indeed he regards both John and Jesus as outstanding personalities, even astonishingly so, and his sympathies are enlisted for them because he thinks they have both been most unjustly done to death. His attitude is thus in general that of a friendly Jewish outsider—a very difficult part for a convinced Christian to play without betraying himself in some fashion as a believer in the full Christian claims. He, however, nowhere asserts that Jesus was the Messiah. Frey's main contention, then, following Seeberg, is that the writer worked on Jewish general popular oral sources; in other words, he had at his disposal traditions proximate to the occurrences, and therefore worthy of attention as giving a picture of an early outside view of nascent Christianity.

Seeberg thinks that Christian manipulation must be admitted in three or four places; but Frey tries to show that he is here mistaken. Frey is perhaps not sufficiently cautious in thus leaving no loophole. But even with this qualification, if the main contention of both scholars can stand, the possibility of our being faced with early external traditions of some kind is a matter of quite extraordinary interest, and deserves the careful attention of all students of Christian beginnings.

As practically nothing is known of these passages by English readers, it may be of service to present those few of them who see this study, with a translation of the German version of these eight extracts. They may then judge for themselves how the contents strike them. But whatever may be their opinion as to their value or worthlessness, it cannot be denied that every scrap of material, however intractible, that can be held by any trained mind to contain the possibility of having even the remotest bearing on the surroundings of earliest Christianity, possesses a unique interest and fascination of its own; for the first century is otherwise practically silent outside the New Testament documents.

The version that follows is made from the German translation given in Frey's volume; I have, however, added the sub-titles. It is literal and clumsy, like the German, which faithfully follows the Slavonic. The variant readings in the MSS. are slight, and I have not noted them in detail. For the present paper is intended for the general reader solely, and not for the specialist, who must deal at first hand with Frey's technical exposition, which, as far as I am aware, has not yet been disposed of, or indeed in any way answered.

I.

JOHN'S PROCLAMATION AND HIS REBUKE OF THE AUTHORITIES.

(Follows on *B. J.* II. vii. 2.)

1. Now at that time a man went about among the Jews in strange garments; for he had put pelts on his body everywhere where it was not covered with his own hair; 2. indeed to look at he was like a wild man.

3. He came to the Jews and summoned them to freedom, saying: "God hath sent me, that I may show you the way of the Law, wherein ye may free yourselves from many holders of power. 4. And there will be no mortal ruling over you, only the Highest who hath sent me." 5. And when the people had heard this, they were joyful. And there went after him all Judæa, that lies in the region round Jerusalem.

6. And he did nothing else to them save that he plunged them into the stream of the Jordan and dismissed them, instructing them that they should cease from evil works, and [promising] that there would [then] be given them a ruler who would set them free and subject to them all that is not in submission; but no one of whom we speak (?),[1] would himself be subjected. 7. Some reviled, but others got faith.

8. And when he had been brought to Archelaus and the doctors of the Law had assembled, they asked him who he is and where he has been until then. 9. And to this he made answer and spake: "I am pure; [for] the Spirit of God hath led me on, and [I live on] cane and roots and tree-food.[2] 10. But when they threatened to put him to torture if he would not cease from those words and deeds, he nevertheless said: "It is meet for *you* [rather] to cease from your heinous works and cleave unto the Lord your God."

11. And there rose up in anger Simon, an Essæan by extraction, a scribe, and he spake: "We read every day the divine books. 12. But thou, only now come from the forest like a wild animal,—*thou* darest in sooth to teach *us* and to mislead the people with thy reprobate words." 13. And he rushed forward to do him bodily violence. 14. But he, rebuking them, spake: "I will not disclose to you the mystery which dwelleth in you, for ye have not desired it. 15. Thereby an untold calamity is come upon you, and because of yourselves."

16. And when he had thus spoken, he went forth to the other

---

[1] This is uncertain. It seems to mean "no one who had ceased from evil works." This clause, however, which comes at the end of the sentence in the Slavonic, may belong to the next sentence; in which case it would read: "At his words some reviled, etc." (p. 33, n. 1).

[2] Ger. *Holzspäne*, 'chips,' 'shavings,'—a quite impossible meaning. It occurs again at the end of § III.

side of the Jordan; and while no one durst rebuke him, that one did what [he had done] also heretofore.

II.

HIS INTERPRETATION OF PHILIP'S DREAM.

(Follows on *B. J.* II. ix. 1.)

1. While Philip was [still] in possession of his dominion, he saw a dream,—how an eagle tore out both his eyes. 2. And he summoned all his wise men. 3. But when each interpreted the dream differently, there came to him suddenly, without being summoned, that man of whom we have previously written, that he went about in skins of animals and cleansed the people in the waters of the Jordan. 4. And he spake: "Give ear to the word of the Lord,—the dream which thou hast seen. 5. The eagle—that is thy venality; because that bird is violent and rapacious. 6. And that sin will take away thy eyes—which are thy dominion and thy wife." 7. And when he had thus spoken, Philip died before evening and his dominion was given to Agrippa.

III.

HIS PERSISTENT REBUKING OF AGRIPPA AND HIS EXECUTION.

(Follows immediately on the preceding.)

1. And Herod, his brother, took his wife Herodias. 2. And because of her all the doctors of the Law abhorred him, but durst not accuse him before his face.

3. But only that one whom they called a wild man, came to him in anger and spake: "Why hast thou taken the wife of thy brother? 4. As thy brother hath died a death void of pity, thou too wilt be reaped off by the heavenly sickle. 5. God's decree will not be silenced, but will destroy thee through evil affliction in foreign lands. 6. For thou dost not raise up seed for thy brother, but gratifiest thy fleshly lust and committest adultery, seeing that four children of him are alive."

7. Now when Herod heard [this], he was filled with wrath and commanded that they should beat him and drive him away. 8. But he accused Herod incessantly wherever he found him, and

right up to the time when he (H.) put him under arrest and gave orders to slay him.

9. Now his disposition (or character) was extraordinary and his mode of life not that of a man; indeed just like a bodiless spirit, thus did this one too continue. 10. His lips knew no bread; not even at Easter [? orig. Passover] did he taste unleavened bread, saying that, in remembrance of God who had freed the people from slavery, it was given for eating in the flight, for the way was in haste. To wine and intoxicating drink he let himself not even draw near. And every animal he abhorred [as food], and every wrong he rebuked, and tree-produce served him for use.

IV.

THE MINISTRY, TRIAL AND CRUCIFIXION OF JESUS.

(Follows on *B. J.* II. ix. 3.)

1. At that time also a man came forward,—if even it is fitting to call him a man [simply]. 2. His nature as well as his form were a man's; but his showing forth was more than [that] of a man. 3. His works, that is to say, were godly, and he wrought wonder-deeds amazing and full of power. 4. Therefore it is not possible for me to call him a man [simply]. 5. But again, looking at the existence he shared with all, I would also not call him an angel.

6. And all that he wrought through some kind of invisible power, he wrought by word and command.

7. Some said of him, that our first Lawgiver has risen from the dead and shows forth many cures and arts. 8. But others supposed [less definitely] that he is sent by God.

9. Now he opposed himself in much to the Law and did not observe the Sabbath according to ancestral custom. 10. Yet, on the other hand, he did nothing reprehensible nor any crime; but by word solely he effected everything.

11. And many from the folk followed him and received his teachings. 12. And many souls became wavering, supposing that thereby the Jewish tribes would set themselves free from the Roman hands.

13. Now it was his custom often to stop on the Mount of Olives facing the city. 14. And there also he avouched his cures

to the people. 15. And there gathered themselves to him of servants (*Knechten*) a hundred and fifty, but of the folk a multitude.

16. But when they saw his power, that he accomplished everything that he would by word, they urged him that he should enter the city and cut down the Roman soldiers and Pilate and rule over us. 17. But that one scorned it.

18. And thereafter, when knowledge of it came to the Jewish leaders, they gathered together with the High-priest and spake: "We are powerless and weak to withstand the Romans. 19. But as withal the bow is bent, we will go and tell Pilate what we have heard, and we will be without distress, lest if he hear it from others, we be robbed of our substance and ourselves be put to the sword and our children ruined." 20. And they went and told it to Pilate.

21. And he sent and had many of the people cut down. 22. And he had that wonder-doer brought up. And when he had instituted a trial concerning him, he perceived that he is a doer of good, but not an evil-doer, nor a revolutionary, nor one who aimed at power, and set him free. 23. He had, you should know, healed his dying wife.

24. And he went to his accustomed place and wrought his accustomed works. 25. And as again more folk gathered themselves together round him, then did he win glory through his works more than all.

26. The teachers of the Law were [therefore] envenomed with envy and gave thirty talents to Pilate, in order that he should put him to death. 27. And he, after he had taken [the money], gave them consent that they should themselves carry out their purpose.

28. And they took him and crucified him according to the ancestral law.

V.

THE TREATMENT OF THE FIRST CHRISTIANS.

(Follows on *B. J.* II. xi. 6, after the notice on the death of Agrippa.)

1. Again Claudius sent his authorities to those states—Cuspius Fadus and Tiberius Alexander, both of whom kept the

people in peace, not allowing them to depart in anything from the pure laws.

2. But if anyone diverged from the word of the Law, plaint was brought before the teachers of the Law. 3. Often they expelled him and sent him to the Emperor's presence.

4. And at the time of these two many had been discovered as servants of the previously described wonder-doer; and as they spake to the people about their teacher,—that he is living, although he is dead, and that he will free you from your servitude, —many from the folk gave ear to the above-named and took upon themselves their precept,—5. not because of their reputation; they were indeed of the humbler sort some just cobblers, others sandal-makers, others artisans.

6. And [yet] as marvellous signs they accomplished in truth what they would.

7. But when those noble governors saw the misleading of the people, they deliberated with the scribes to seize and put them to death, for fear lest the little be not little if it have ended in the great. 8. But they shrank back and were alarmed over the signs, saying: "In the plain course such wonders do not occur. 9. But if they do not issue from the counsel of God, they will quickly be convicted." 10. And they gave them [the Christians] authority to act as they would.

11. But afterwards, becoming pestered by them, they had them sent away, some to the Emperor, but others to Antioch, others again to distant lands,—for the testing of the matter.

12. But Claudius removed the two governors, [and] sent Cumanus.

VI.

THE TRILINGUAL INSCRIPTION CONCERNING JESUS.
(Inserted in *B. J.* V. v. 2.)

At it (the barrier of the Temple) were columns . . . and on these inscriptions in Greek and Roman and Jewish characters, publishing the law of purity and [proclaiming] that no foreigner should enter the inner [court]; for they called it the Holy [Place] to which one had to ascend by fourteen steps, and whose upper part was built in a square.

And over these tablets with inscriptions hung a fourth tablet with inscription in these [three] characters, to the effect: Jesus has not reigned as king; he has been crucified by the Jews, because he proclaimed the destruction of the city and the laying waste of the temple.

VII.

PORTENTS AT THE DEATH OF JESUS AND RUMOURS OF HIS RESURRECTION.

(Follows on *B. J.* V. v. 4, at the end of the description of the Temple-curtain.)

1. This curtain (*katapetasma*) was prior to this generation entire, because the people were pious; but now it was lamentable to look at. 2. It had, you should know, been suddenly rent from the top to the ground, when they delivered over to death through bribery the doer of good, the man—yea, him who through his doing was no man.

3. And of many other signs they tell which came to pass at that time.

4. And it was said that after he was put to death, yea after burial in the grave, he was not found.

5. Some then assert that he is risen; but others, that he has been stolen by his friends. 6. I, however, do not know which speak more correctly.

7. For a dead man cannot rise of himself—though possibly with the help of another righteous man; unless it (lit. he) will be an angel or another of the heavenly authorities, or God himself appears as a man and accomplishes what he will,—both walks with men and falls, and lies down and rises up, as it is according to his will.

8. But others said that it was not possible to steal him, because they had put guards all round his grave,—thirty Romans, but a thousand Jews.

9. Such [is narrated] as to that curtain (*katapetasma*). Moreover [as to] the cause of its tearing there are [? various statements].

VIII.

A Prophecy concerning Jesus.

(In *B. J.* VI. v. 4, where in our texts the prophecy of the world-ruler is referred to Vespasian solely.)

Some indeed by this understood Herod, but others the crucified wonder-doer Jesus, others again Vespasian.

In conclusion a few very general remarks may be added calling attention to the most salient points.

In the John-pieces (I.-III.) there is nothing sufficiently distinctive to show any literary dependence on the New Testament accounts. On the contrary, there are entire novelties and wide divergences. In the first place the strong political colouring given by the writer to the proclamation of the prophet is quite out of keeping with anything to be found in the Christian presentation. But the most striking difference is the protracted period assigned to John's activity. 'At that time' means during the ethnarchy of Archelaus. Now Herod the Great died in 4 B.C., and Archelaus, who succeeded him, was deposed in 6 A.D. It is quite inconceivable that any Christian writer who had the gospel-story before him, could have made what would be so astounding a statement to Christian ears,—one that would at once appear to the most moderately instructed as an egregious blunder. Surely the last thing an intelligent forger would desire to do would be to give occasion to his readers to call the canonical narrative into question concerning so prominent a feature as John's almost equal age with Jesus, and so practically invite them to dismiss all the graphic details of the birth-stories as fictitious?—unless it be that he wrote before these stories were in circulation. No one short of a lunatic would concoct 'evidence' against his own side. The writer must therefore have moved in circles who would see no difficulty in assigning to John a public activity of at least 30 years; for he tells us that John survived the death of Philip, which took place somewhere between 33 and 36 A.D.

The cross-examination of John by the authorities and the incident of Simon the Essene are also arresting novelties; but there is nothing improbable in them. The introduction of the name Essene does not in any way depend on Christian tradition; for the surprising fact is that, though there are close parallels between some of the doctrines of the Essenes and gospel-ethics, and between some of their practices and the regulations, for instance, laid down for the mission of the apostles and the communal observances of the earliest Christian communities, the New Testament writers never mention the name. The wording of the refusal of John at the end of his rebuke to disclose a certain mystery to his official opponents has led some to the supposition that this is a cryptic reference to Jesus,— meaning 'the mystery dwelling among you.' That of course would be impossible at so early a date as prior to A.D. 6. But surely, quite apart from this, a Christian apologist would have been at pains to bring out clearly so essential a feature as John's acknowledgment of the Messiahship of Jesus, and not go out of his way to disguise it? It is a curious and thought-provoking phrase. It may refer to the 'kingdom,' to the indwelling rule and law of God, that is brought to consciousness in the hearts of the repentant; or it may possibly be that John had some inner mystical doctrine to reveal, for we have to remember that the Mandæan or Gnostic John-tradition, which has come down to our own days, has ever laid the greatest stress on the mystical element in the teaching of the Baptizer.

The interpretation of the dream of Philip, like the stress laid upon John's strange appearance and dress and his extraordinary mode of life, is just such a detail as would strike the imagination and linger in the memory of the people. What more likely and in keeping with precedent than that a prophet should interpret the dream of the king? But here we have, not only a novelty for readers of the gospel-account, but also a contradiction with Josephus himself. The unfavourable character given to Philip, the stress laid on his 'venality,' is in complete contrast with the reputation given him by Josephus in his *Antiquities* (XVIII. iv. 6), where he is praised for the mild and peaceable disposition he displayed in his government, and for the personal interest he took in the administration of justice. Now the *Antiquities* was completed in 93/94 A.D. Had then our writer known it, he would not presumably have made Josephus contradict himself so egregiously. This raises the question as to the possibility of his having written before the *Antiquities* got into wide circulation.

Piece III. in some respects agrees with and in others differs from the synoptic account of the marriage of Herod Antipas, tetrarch of Galilee and Peræa, with the wife (Slav. Jos. widow) of his brother Philip. But Josephus himself in his *Antiquities* (XVIII. v. 1 and 4) tells the story quite differently from both. There we read that Herodias was married first of all to Herod Boëthus, and that the wife of Philip was Salome, the daughter of this union; so that Philip was son-in-law of Herodias. Herod Antipas, says Josephus, was the second husband of Herodias, and the marriage took place while the first husband, Boëthus, was still alive. Josephus, moreover, says that Philip died childless; while our author avers that he left four children surviving him. Moreover Josephus in the famous passage concerning John in the *Antiquities* (XVIII. v. 2) knows nothing of John's execution being due to so personal a cause as is depicted both by the gospels and our author, though very differently; it is in the *Antiquities* ascribed solely to Antipas' apprehension of the political consequences of the John-movement. Our author is then clearly ignorant of both the *Antiquities*-account and also of the most characteristic feature of the gospel-narrative, the graphic story of the dancing of the daughter of Herodias. Everything therefore goes to show that he is drawing on some other traditional source.

Finally, as the climax to John's extraordinary scruples about food, it is asserted that he would not touch unleavened bread even at Passover-time,—an absolutely obligatory observance in Jewry. Moreover he is made to give an exegetical justification for his abstention. This is the distinctive touch of a Jewish hand; it is exceedingly unlikely that it would ever have occurred to a late Christian.

As to the John-pieces then we seem to be moving in a thoroughly Jewish atmosphere, and there is nothing characteristically Christian about them.

The Jesus-pieces (IV. and VI. to VIII.) are naturally the most arresting and form the main *crux* of the whole matter. It seems to be generally held that all the eight pieces are by the same hand. They may be said to have in general the same terms of expression, to breathe the same spirit and present similar characteristics. In the main Jesus-pieces the author makes a show of trying to get at a reasonable point of view; but he hesitates in his judgment and frankly confesses his inability to make up his mind. He is convinced that the more generally credible events themselves are historic; but as to the sheerly miraculous elements he is content to set them forth as rumours giving rise to absolutely contradictory opinions. So non-committal and rationalistic a proceeding is quite foreign to the mentality of a convinced Christian. This attitude of reserve and the very striking divergences of the writer from the gospel-accounts are in the sharpest possible distinction to the perspective and procedure of the compilers of such apocryphal documents as the *Acts of Pilate* and *The Gospel of Peter*. In the latter the literary dependence on the gospels is manifest on all hands; what is added is in no way contradictory, but adduced solely to exalt the greatness of Jesus and heighten the impression of the miraculous element.

If piece IV. is carefully and critically compared with the famous spurious passage concerning Jesus in our text of the *Antiquities* (XVIII. iii. 3), it will at once be seen that if there is any possible question of dependence between them, it is not on the side of our author. Even among the opinions he cites, there is no hint of Messiahship. When he says that some "supposed that he had been sent by God," it means no more than what he makes John assert of himself,—namely, that he was a prophet. It seems to me moreover highly improbable that any late Christian could have referred to his Lord, the one and only Son of God, as 'that wonder-doer' or the 'crucified wonder-doer Jesus.'

The divergences from the gospel-account of the Jesus-story are so striking that they need not be dwelt on. To every instructed Christian the gospel-narratives are presumably so familiar in all their details, that the contradictions with our author's account will present themselves automatically. Nevertheless the more one meditates on the account in piece IV. of the typical external acts of the ministry and the intrigues of the Jewish authorities to compass the death of Jesus, the more does it seem within its own measures not to be inconsistent; in fact it hangs very well together from an outside point of view. That view is in no way due to a manipulation of gospel-information; it is based on very different data, and has all the appearance of an honest attempt to piece together and interpret floating traditions and conjectures reflected from days contemporaneous perchance with the attempts of the 'many' to set forth the events, as the introduction to the Lukan gospel informs us.

The phrase 'servants' as applied to the disciples, it may be noted, is a thoroughly Jewish conception; it was used by the Rabbis to emphasize the relationship between pupils and teacher. The precise figure 150 may be a round number; otherwise it depends on a tradition for which the 12 and the 70 were of no importance.

The final sentence, which avers, not only that the Jewish authorities themselves crucified Jesus, but that this was in accordance with the Law, is so astonishing in the latter respect that it has been set down to a gross blunder of the Slavonic translator from the Greek original, which may have read 'contrary to the

Law'—κατὰ with the genitive and not the accusative. This seems a reasonable supposition; though we must remember that Jewish rulers in Maccabæan days did crucify their political opponents.

The trilingual inscription statement (VI.) is a wild piece of fanciful combination. The writer has heard of an inscription connected with the execution of Jesus; indeed it was required by law that the formal charge should be placarded in all cases of capital punishment. Moreover he has heard that this particular notice was set forth in three languages; and he also has heard that there were trilingual inscriptions outside the inner court of the Temple. In combining the two he departs so far from his general sobriety that we might almost think the passage was by another hand; but this is otherwise not probable. The first charge against Jesus was that he had excited the people to revolt; of this he was acquitted by Pilate. The authorities had then to give some other excuse: Jesus was executed not because of any Messianistic agitation, but because he prophesied disaster to the temple and the holy city. Some excuse had to be found that would placate the people.

In piece VII. the rending of the veil and the reference to many other portents seem to depend on characteristically Christian tradition; but it need not be supposed that this tradition was in the fixed gospel-form in which we now have it. The phrase 'prior to this generation' is intended to mean some 30/40 years before Josephus wrote his History (75-79 A.D.). It is interesting to note that at that time similar portents were in the air; for Jewish tradition (the Talmuds and Josephus himself, *B.J.* VI. v. 3) makes mention of a mysterious spontaneous opening of the heavy iron temple-doors 40 years before the destruction of Jerusalem, and the *Gospel of the Hebrews* refers to a similarly mysterious breach in the iron threshold of the same doors. There were widespread legends of portents current in the folk-memory. Our author then goes on to treat of the rumours and contradictory statements about the resurrection; and here, as before, he ruminates on possibilities, giving the conjectural pros and cons, but declining to commit himself on the side of the most vital belief of Christendom.

Piece V., concerning the early Christians, is equally as far from literary dependence on the canonical Acts as are the Jesus-pieces on the Gospels. There are wide divergences; and the whole produces an impression of utter ignorance of the detailed, methodical setting-forth of the thirty years of history contained in the Acts. Isolated facts, such as Paul's being sent to Cæsar at Rome, are absurdly generalized on the one hand, and on the other the events of decades are crammed into the narrow time-frame of some four years, the period of office of the two governors mentioned (44-48 A.D.). The phrase "But if they do not issue from the counsel of God, they will quickly be convicted" is thought by some to indicate literary dependence on a similar saying in the Acts. But the latter famous utterance, ascribed to Gamaliel (prior to 7 A.D.), is worded so very differently that, if any connection between them can be supposed, it may well be ascribed in both cases to the uncertain echoing in the popular mind of a well-known Rabbinical pronouncement.

In conclusion, then, it may be said that the hope of extracting anything of value out of these astonishing and puzzling interpolations depends on establishing the reasonableness of the hypothesis, that they are based on echoes of popular traditions still floating about in the Jewish environment of Christianity in, say, the last third of the first century. There is, I think, much that goes to show the likelihood of this supposal, or at least to deter us from summarily dismissing it. But even if we are persuaded to this extent, we are confronted with the still more difficult task of imagining a satisfactory conjecture as to the status and motive of the writer.

If we hold him to have been a Jew, as the above analysis seems to require, what plausible motive can we ascribe to him for interpolating the matter into the text of Josephus? Was he a disinterested lover of history who thought that Josephus had fallen short of historical impartiality by neglecting to mention two such remarkable personages as John and Jesus and two such important movements as those associated with their names, and desired to amend the historian in this respect in days when copyright had not yet been dreamed of? Or may we assume that a pupil of Josephus would think himself entitled to amend the narrative?

If, on the contrary, he was a Christian, the interest in filling the gaps would be easily understandable, had he based himself on canonical tradition. But the divergences from and flat contradictions of that tradition are so extraordinary, that one is all the time kept asking in astonishment: What sort of a Christian could this man ever have been?

To have succeeded in producing such an impression designedly argues the procedure of a mind of such extraordinary subtlety and psychological dexterity that it is too uncanny for credence. Any deliberate attempt of this kind would surely have betrayed itself in some way; but as a matter of fact there is no indication of subtle manipulation of gospel-data anywhere. It is not only very difficult but entirely out of the question to think that any late Christian forger could have thus deliberately challenged the firmly established canonical tradition on so many points. Therefore if the writer were a Christian, he must have been a first-century man; that is to say he wrote before the Greek canonical gospels were in general circulation or at any rate before they had penetrated to his environment.

There remains only one other possible conjecture —from which everybody has so far instinctively shrunk: Can the writer after all have been Josephus himself? But if so, why does he contradict himself so flatly,— to say nothing of the difficulty of conjecturing his motive for cutting out the passages?

It thus appears that, whatever hypothesis of authorship we make—whether Christian, Jew or Josephus, we are left floundering in a welter of inconsistencies; all that can be said is that the Jew alternative is the least improbable.

And there we must leave this baffling problem, in the hope that our readers will at any rate be interested in having it brought to their notice; for in any case these passages must be considered striking curiosities, even perhaps the greatest to be found, in the ancient literature that is generally classed under the caption— 'Christian forgeries.'

IV.

THE FOURTH GOSPEL PROEM:
A NEW VERSION VENTURE.

CONNECTION.

AFTER I had for some time been making a close study of Lidzbarski's translations of the Mandæan John-Book and Liturgies, I had occasion in another connection to refer to the Greek text (Westcott & Hort) of the prologue to the fourth gospel. As I read, I found that a number of Mandæan associations came welling up from the preconscious, especially with regard to Life and Light, the use of the term Man and the way the sentences about John the Baptist linked on to these concepts. I found I was almost automatically construing parts of this familiar text from a new angle or at any rate envisaging them in a new perspective. I had already for long been convinced that the historical references broke awkwardly into the doctrinal proem proper, and that this contained what may be called some characteristic general gnostic notions. Moreover I had long been of the opinion that the proem was based on a 'source'; but thought that this 'source' was most probably already in Greek when it was made such deft use of by the inspired writer of the 'pneumatic' gospel. I now asked myself, could it possibly have been originally in Aramaic, for there are indubitably some strained constructions in it, that might be explicable as literal renderings of Semitic idioms. Translation into Greek would doubtless make the original appear to be more hellenistically coloured than was actually the case and so 'philosophize' it somewhat. The main difficulty seemed to lie in determining what could have been the Semitic original of the leading term rendered by *Logos*? Was it Word or Wisdom or some other Divine Power or Potency? On this I could form no conclusion. But further, whatever it was, could it have been translated by any other Greek term than *Logos*? For the student of comparative Hellenistic theology is not confined to seeking for parallels or associations with the idea behind this term in Stoicism and Philo simply; he has to take into consideration a far wider field of research. In the Trismegistic literature, for instance, in which the Heavenly Man doctrine is prominent, the parallel notion is rendered by *Noûs*, Mind, and in the Hellenistic poem so beloved by the Later Platonists and generally known as the 'Chaldæan Oracles,'[1] the Mind of the Father stands at the summit; while in allied Gnostic tradition connected with the 'Chaldæan Mysteries' or even said to be based on the 'Chaldæan Books,' where again the Divine Man doctrine is prominent, the term preferred is Mind. Mind, moreover, in the Valentinian system stands at the head of the Plērōma. This is solely with regard to translation into Greek in the general Hellenistic theological language of the time, and says nothing about the Semitic or Chaldæan original terms, which may have been numerous, apart from the very general (notably Egyptian) Oriental magical notion of creation by the word. Certainly the Man-doctrine was wide-spread and where personifications were the order of the day, Man and Mind would go better together than Man and Word or Reason or even Wisdom. It is, however, with all hesitation that I have ventured to use the term Mind in my transla-

[1] See my 'Echoes from the Gnosis' series, vols. viii. and ix., *The Chaldæan Oracles*, London, 1908.

tion, and more to call attention to the problem than anything else.

With these ideas—namely the supposal of a probable Aramaic original of the proem-source and the consequent 'philosophizing' by translation into Hellenistic Greek of some terms that in the original were more concretely presented, I attempted the following version. This I did before I had read Prof. C. F. Burney's recent (1922) arresting study, entitled *The Aramaic Origin of the Fourth Gospel* (Oxford, The Clarendon Press). The contention of the Professor of the Interpretation of Holy Scripture at Oxford, who is so great an authority on the O.T., is that not only for the proem but for much, if not the whole, of the gospel there is an Aramaic background. Whatever may be ultimately decided on this novel and far-reaching hypothesis, it should inaugurate a fruitful line of N.T. research. My own venture is far more modest in every way; I deal with a single 'source' only, and have not the competence to treat even that technically from the Semitic side. The only remark I would venture to make on Prof. Burney's labours is in respect to the Johannine *Greek* quotations from the O.T. The problem whether the few of them which differ from the LXX. Greek Targum or Translation,—the Authorised Version of the time so to say,—were made freshly from the Hebrew, does not seem to me necessarily to help to prove the author's contention. They are far more likely to have been taken from what is said to have been probably the earliest Christian Greek document, —a collection of proof-texts to establish the claims of Christian Messianism from O.T. prophecy, at times not without accommodation. They sometimes agree with and sometimes diverge from the Septuagint rendering

All this has been most thoroughly worked out by Proff. Rendel Harris and Vacher Burch in their indispensable work (Pt. I., 1916, Pt. II., 1920) on the now famous Testimony Book (*Testimonia contra Judæos*).

I also conjectured, presumably owing to the rhythms of the Mandæan books running in my head, that the 'source' might have been in verse; and found that the Greek broke up easily into some sort of rhythmic lines. But of course this was pure guess-work on my part. Professor Burney, however, with his wide knowledge of Hebrew and Palestinian Aramaic, has come most definitely to this conclusion as to the proem. If the rest of the gospel cannot be so treated, this seems to me to be an additional indication that in the prologue we are dealing with a 'source.' Though my tentative translation from the Greek differs both in analysis and phrasing from Prof. Burney's, I so far see no compelling reason to alter the phrasing by his, and let the breaking up of the lines stand to indicate rhythm rather than the measured lines he has so ingeniously endeavoured to reconstruct into Aramaic.

TRANSLATION.

1. In Beginning[1] was Mind;[2]

[1] In the original this was probably the usual cosmological formula 'in the beginning.' The Greek may suggest a more metaphysical meaning and the Vulgate Latin seems to continue the process, for *principium* might carry the meaning of 'primality'; cp. Cicero, *Tusc.* i. 23, 54: "There is no origin of primality (*principii*); for it is out of primality that all things originate"; Tertullian, *Adv. Hermog.* 19: "In Greek the term primality, namely ἀρχή, takes the primacy (*principatum*), not only in the category of order (*ordinativum*), but also in that of potency (*potestivum*)."

[2] If there is any Mandæan term with which to seek a parallel it might perhaps be Mānā, which seems generally to mean Mind. Prof. Rendel Harris, in his illuminating study of the Proem, would make the original of Logos 'Wisdom' (Ḥokhmah), and brings forward some striking quotations from the O.T. sapiential literature and Patristic commentaries in justification. This Hebrew (O.T.) and Greek (Apocryphal) Wisdom-literature is clearly influenced Hellenistically, and the equation Logos=Sophia in the *Gk. version* of the 4th gospel is of great interest. In addition to R. H.'s *Origin of the Prologue to St. John's Gospel*, see his interesting paper 'Athena,

And Mind was with GOD.[1]

2. So[2] Mind was God.

This[3] was in Beginning with GOD.

3. All kept coming into existence[4] through[5] it[6];

And apart from it came into existence not a single [thing].

4. What has come into existence in it[7] was Life;[8]

And LIFE[9] was the Light of the [true] Men.[10]

5. And the Light shineth in the Darkness;

And the Darkness did not emprison[11] it.

Sophia and the Logos,' pp. 56-72 of the *Bulletin* of the John Rylands Library, Manchester, July, 1922. It may be objected that 'Word' is to be preferred, seeing that in the Targums Memrah=the Creative Word, Logos; but my contention is that the Greek Noûs is nearer to the Deity than the Greek Logos.

[1] The Gk. phrase πρὸς τὸν θεόν is a grammatical puzzle; this is, however, probably solved by the hypothesis of a literal translation from a Semitic original. The Gnostic Heracleon (2nd cent.), the first known commentator on the fourth gospel, who was apparently ignorant of Semitics, conjectured that ἡνωμένος ('at-one-with,' 'in-co-adunition-with') should be supplied; others think the phrase is Hellenistic (Koinē) for παρὰ τῷ θεῷ—*i.e.*, 'along with,' 'by the side of,' or simply 'with' God. In the Greek text ὁ θεός is distinguished (and I think deliberately), by the prefixing of the definite article, from the following simple θεός. But 'The God' is clumsy in English, and so I resort to the type-trick of capitalization to mark the distinction.

[2] The Gk. καί renders probably a Semitic particle that serves several other purposes than that of a purely copulative function.

[3] *Sc.* Mind or God, not as a second God, but as the Divine or Creative Intelligence of GOD.

[4] Or 'continued to become' (impf.),—the idea of 'perpetual creation.'

[5] The Old Syriac versions (*e.g.* C.) read 'in' and not 'through'; see F. C. Burkitt, *Evangelion da-Mepharreshe: The Curetonian Version of the Four Gospels, with the Readings of the Sinai Palimpsest and the Early Syriac Patristic Evidence* (Cambridge, 1904), i. 423. The Old (*i.e.* pre-Peshīttā) Syriac versions should be a great help in determining the Aram. original, as the two dialects are closely related.

[6] *Sc.* Mind.

[7] *Sc.* Mind.

[8] That would be the Mandæan Second Life.

[9] Or 'The Life'—the same distinction as with the terms for 'God.'

[10] The article cannot be neglected; it signifies those who are really Men, *i.e.* conscious members of the celestial or angelic humanity or true Race. All this connects with the *Anthrōpos*-doctrine of the Gnosis. Man (the Aram. idiom 'Son of Man,' if translated literally, is misleading in Gk.) is the Celestial or Primal Man, Adam Qadmon. As Thrice-greatest Hermes says, the vast majority of mortals are not worthy to be called 'Men'; all men have Reason, but few as yet have Mind (*i.e.* are spiritual). The true Men who have the Light of Life are the Prophets and Perfect.

Suppress,' 'hold back,' 'detain.' Burney has 'obscured it not.'

([1]There was a Man sent by God,—his name Yōánes This [Man] came for bearing witness, that he might bear witness about the Light, in order that all [men] might have faith through it. That [Man] was not the Light, but [came] in order that he might bear witness about the Light.)

6. It was the True Light,
   Which enlighteneth every Man[2]
   Who cometh into the world.[3]
7. It was in the world;
   And the world kept coming into existence through it[4];
   And the world did not know it.[5]
8. It came unto its own;[6]
   And its own did not receive it.
9. But as many as received it,
   To them it gave power[7]
   To become Children of God,[8]—
10. To those who have faith in his name,[9]—

---

[1] This paragraph seems clearly to be an interpolation into, or overworking of, his original 'source' by the writer, or perhaps part compiler, of the fourth gospel.

[2] Prophet or Divine Messenger.

[3] *This* world (Gk. κόσμος, Heb. *tebel*, Mand. *tibil*); there were other worlds according to the Mandā or Gnōsis. 'This world' in the sense of the earth; the world in the wider meaning would be the Heb. '*olam*.

[4] *Sc.* the Light, *i.e.* the Life of Mind.

[5] If the reader prefers to personify the Light and its synonyms, he can substitute 'him' for 'it'; and so also in the following phrases.

[6] *Sc.* creations (n.pl.), world and other creations up or down to man; cp. Jn. xix. 27, where the 'disciple whom he loved' is said to have taken the Mother 'unto his own' (εἰς τὰ ἴδια), which is generally supposed to mean 'his own home.' 'Its own' therefore signifies 'habitations.' The following 'its own' (m.pl.) refers to the 'inhabitants.'

[7] *Sc.* spiritual power—lit. 'allowance,' 'possibility,' generally translated 'authority'; it is not physical power (δύναμις, 'lordship,' 'domination'), but moral power—'grace.'

[8] That is of Mind.

[9] That is who have faith in the still higher Power (the mystic 'Name' or Soul, or Mind, or Primality) of Great Life—GOD.

Who were brought to birth,
Not out of [the blending of] bloods,[1]
11. Nor of urge[2] of flesh,
Nor of urge of a male,—
But out of God.
12. So[3] Mind became flesh[4]
And tabernacled[5] in us,[6]—
13. And we beheld its glory,
Glory as of [? an] only-begotten[7] from Father,—
Full[8] of Delight[9] and Truth.

([10]Yōánēs beareth witness about him,[11] and hath cried aloud, saying—he it was who said—: He who

---

[1] That is, of earthly parents; for they were born from Above, i.e. were spiritual births.

[2] It means 'wish' rather than 'will'—'desire,' 'urge.'

[3] Lit. 'and' (καί); but clearly meaning 'by such birth from above.'

[4] This seems to mean simply 'was enfleshed.' The Old Syriac has 'body,' not 'flesh'; so also in 11.

[5] Lit. 'pitched its tent'; this refers to the extended *shekīnah*-doctrine. In the Mandæan tradition *škīnā* is the frequently-recurring technical term for the 'dwelling,' 'housing,' 'tenting,' or 'spiritual body' or 'glory,' of the celestials—the *ūthrā's* or 'treasures' or perhaps 'fulnesses' (lit. 'riches'). Burney has: "And set his *shekīntā* among us," referring solely to Yeshū' Messiah. *Shekīntā* is Palestinian Aramaic for Heb. *shekīnah*.

[6] Namely the Prophets or Perfect.

[7] *Mono-genēs*,—this in pre- and post-Christian Gnostic tradition is the general technical term for 'born,' 'emanated' or 'created' from a 'single' source (μονο-), i.e. one-and-only parent, and is used of spiritual beings who are superior to the conditions of sex-generation. Cp. the *perikopē* on Melchi Sedek (King of Peace, Prince of Righteousness) in Heb. vii. 1-21. He is there said to be "father-less, mother-less, [earthly] genealogy-less, without beginning of days or end of life, but made-in-the-likeness of GOD'S Son." In common speech *monogenēs* is usually found as meaning the only one of a kind; if only one daughter has been born to a man, she would be characterized as *monogenēs*. But the vulgar tongue is *not* the language of mysticism. In the above-referred to article (p. 123) Prof. Rendel Harris thinks that the meaning of *monogenēs* as 'child of one parent only,' as applied to Athena born from the head of Zeus, which he suggests, but rejects, is a 'quite new' idea; but I have been insisting on it for a score of years at least. He would render it as 'darling,' but this is really too *bourgeois*.

[8] This picks up Mind in 12₁; it is m. sing.

[9] The root-meaning of χάρις.

[10] This is the second redactorial interpolation or overworking.

[11] The Greek translator unquestionably understood this as referring to Yeshū' Messiah. But the puzzling phrasing of the quotation from the Baptist *logoi*-tradition—'my First'—seems to require 'it' instead of 'him,' viz., the Mind-Life-Light of the 'source,' as in the first interpolation.

cometh behind me hath been before me,¹ for he was my First.²)

14. For of its Fulness³ we all received,
    And Delight over against Delight.⁴

(⁵In that the Law (Torah) was given by Moses, Delight and Truth kept coming into the word through Yeshū' Messiah.⁶

No man hath seen God at any time;⁷

An only-begotten <god>, who is in⁸ the bosom⁹ of the Father,—he dictated.)¹⁰

¹ Cp. L. and S. Lex. *s.v.* ἔμπροσθεν: "The *future* is unseen and was therefore regarded as *behind* us, whereas the *past* is known and therefore *before* our eyes."

² Inexplicable in the usual translation, but it might refer to First Life in Mandæan tradition.

³ Or *plērōma* picking up the 'full' of 13a.

⁴ This seems to me to be a distinct reference to the Gnostic notion of pairs or syzygies in the Plērōma; cp. the "Hence pairing with each other (ἀντιστοιχοῦντες)" of the *Apophasis* ascribed to Simon Magus (Hippolytus, *Ref.* vi. 18). The term is used by Xenophon (*Ana.* v. 4, 12) of two bands of dancers facing each other in rows or pairs (see my *Simon Magus*, 1892, p. 20).

⁵ The third interpolation or overworking of the 'source.'

⁶ Ἰησοῦς Χριστός—Yēsūs Hristos. I have, however, kept what I hold to be the Heb.-Aram. original name-combination. It means the Anointed Saviour or Liberator—that is Saviour or Vindicator anointed by the Divine Spirit or Creative and Perfecting Life of God; cp. the O.T. Joshua (LXX. Jesus).

⁷ Cp. the Jewish Gnostic commentator of the Naassene Document, quoting from a prior 'scripture,' or an oral 'logos' ('what was spoken'): "His voice we heard, but his form we have not seen." (See my analysis of this very important Gnostic Document in *Thrice-greatest Hermes*, London, 1906, in Prolegomena, § 'The Myth of Man in the Mysteries'; the quotation is to be found in i. 169.) Compare with this Jn. v. 37: "Ye have never at any time heard his voice, nor have ye seen his form," addressed to the Jews in general; whereas the Naassene quotation refers to the Perfect. This is very important, for if my analysis of the NN. document, which Hippolytus copied, is correct, the Jewish mystic, who commented on the Hellenistic source, was in all probability contemporary with Philo (c. 30 B.C.—45 A.D.), and therefore we have here an indication of another 'source' of the fourth gospel (of which there may have been a number).

⁸ The Gk. ὁ ὢν εἰς τὸν κόλπον ('*into* the bosom') is grammatically impossible: it must rest on a Semitic idiom. The Old Syriac (C.) has Son *from* the bosom of the Father.

⁹ Cp. the Commentary of Ephraim Syrus, which runs: "The Word of the Father came from His bosom, and clothed itself with a body in another bosom; from bosom to bosom it went forth, and pure bosoms have been filled from it: blessed is He who dwelleth in us!" (Burkitt, *op. cit.*, ii. 140).

¹⁰ Namely the gospel which follows; the verb has no object. The Gk. ἐξηγήσατο means also 'related in full,' 'set forth'; the Mandæan technical term is 'discoursed.'

AFTERWORD.

THE legend-like Mandæan tradition concerning the person of John and the distinctive gnostic type of doctrine which it associates with him could by no means have been deduced from, or expanded out of, the bare external historical facts reported by the classical Josephus; it differs moreover in many ways from the more detailed story of the Gospels and their perspective of his doctrinal and prophetical activity. As to the graphic picture of the Gospels, which suggests the sudden arising of a solitary wild figure unconnected with any community or order, a feature so strongly stressed also by the Slavonic Josephus,—the Mandæan handing-on is completely silent. It gives no hint of any peculiarity of this nature in John's dress, much less of any uncouthness in his appearance; indeed, though it makes no statement, it would lead us to infer that John was clad in white, and in all other respects presented little of the wild features of a desert-bred, skin-clad eremite. The classical Josephus is also silent on this popular trait. That John was a prophet, all these accounts are agreed; that he baptized, all are agreed. That he suffered a martyr's death, Josephus and the Gospels are agreed; but strange to say, the Mandæan tradition has not a word on so important and tragical an event. It is difficult to believe that the Mandæan Nazōræans could have been ignorant of the way in which their great prophet met his end; for had they believed he was not executed by Antipas, they would in all probability have contradicted in their own fashion the report of the Jews and Christians in this respect.

This omission of all reference to the death of John would be incomprehensible, did we not reflect in the first place that no attempt is made in the existing Mandæan documents to give anything that could be called a 'Life' of John, and conjecture in the second that in all probability nothing of doctrinal importance was attached to the way of his ending as it was in the case of Jesus. It is of course supposable that there may have been at one time documents of greater detail and more historical value relating to John, which have since fallen into oblivion owing to the focussing of interest on the more plastic material of psychical legend and mystical reverie; but conjecture cannot restore them.

Though in the present restricted exposition no attempt is made to treat the comparative side of the subject, owing to the regrettable fact that we are still without the scientific translation of the main and oldest deposit of the Mandæan scriptures, it may be noted that there are fragmentary traditions on other lines that would make both Dositheus and Simon the Magian disciples of John. Now Dositheus (Dousis or Dosthai) was the precursor of Simon; and the latter was held by the heresiological Church Fathers to be the *fons et origo* of gnosticism, which he certainly was not, but only one of many of the time with already a long heredity behind them. It is to be further noted that the distinctive Simonian school or tradition, which was in no sense Christian, continued at least well on into the third century, and that the Dositheans, who were equally non-Christians, are known of as being numerous even in the sixth century.[1] By the rumour that these Gnostic teachers were 'disciples of John' we must understand in general, I believe, that there was simply in some respects similarity of doctrine betwen them. These Dosthai-Simon legends and reports are associated with early Ebionite controversies (underlying the Pseudo-Clementine romances), and the doctrines involved in them link up with similar notions found in the wide-spread pre-Christian syncretisms, and even universalizing attempts, of many kinds of saving-cults of both a popular and restricted apocalyptic and gnostical character, common to such plainly distinguishable types as the Persian, Chaldæan, and Aramæan religious complexes of the early Hellenistic period. The mass of detailed research work which has been done chiefly in the last generation on Babylonian, Iranian, Syrian, Aramæan, Egyptian and East Mediterranean religious endeavours, whether Hellenistically tinged or otherwise, which flourished so luxuriously during the three centuries before our era and continued to do so in their various ways for the following three centuries and some of them far later, is beginning to make an impression outside the ranks of the specialists, and compelling the attention of the general historian. It is coming to be seen that the unprejudiced evaluation of these many endeavours and movements and the getting of them into a proper perspective constitute an indispensable task for those who would trace the religious features, phases and fortunes of 'world history' in the main moments of its development, and especially those of them which most strongly influenced Western culture in its later formative periods.

[1] See my *Fragments of a Faith Forgotten* (London, 2nd ed., 1906), pp. 162 ff.

We have recently had presented to us an arresting, if provocative, attempt of this kind in Oswald Spengler's *Downfall of the West*. Its two stout volumes of some 1,200 pages have been very widely read in Germany and by knowers of German, and the work has been much discussed and criticized. For naturally specialists and authorities cannot easily brook the incursions into their distinctive territories of a free lance with a knack of, or even genius for, recognizing underlying similar tendencies where previously for the most part the more superficial distinctions have been stressed into fundamental differences. It is true that where so wide a field is surveyed, it is not difficult to catch up such an historical innovator on numerous points of detail, but on the other hand his method certainly does at times enable the reader to fix his attention on the wood rather than on the trees and on the great rivers rather than on the streamlets. We do not, perhaps naturally enough, see eye to eye with Spengler throughout, but here we are not considering his work as a whole. He is referred to because he is the first general historian and philosopher of history who has brought the Mandæans into the picture; and in this he seems, in our judgment, to have got them into a tolerably proper perspective. It may be mentioned also that it was only after the whole of the preceding matter had been written that I read Spengler's work, and that for many years I have been regarding the phenomena of pre-Christian Gnosticism and allied movements from more or less the same angle. It may then be of interest to reproduce Spengler's boldly sketched picture of the conditions in which the heredity of the pre-Christian Gnosis is to be sought and of the apocalyptic eschatological expectations and hopes of salvation that preceded the birth of Christianity.[1]

"What lay in the prophetical religions (Persian, Chaldæan, Jewish) as a presage or presentiment, what at the time of Alexander the Great emerged in metaphysical outlines, was now brought to completion. And this completion aroused in tremendous strength the primitive feeling of nervous dread. It pertains to the last mysteries of humanity and of free-moving life in general that the birth of the I and the birth of world-dread are one and the same; that a macrocosm is spread out before a microcosm,—vast, overwhelming, an abyss of foreign, light-shot being and activity that makes the tiny, solitary self shrink back timorously into itself. Such fear of their own consciousness as from time to time suddenly overwhelms children, is experienced again by no grown-up even in the darkest hours of his life. This deadly fear, however, oppressed the dawning of the new culture. In this morn of the 'magic' world-consciousness, that was faint-hearted, uncertain, obscure about itself, a new glance was taken at the near end of the world. This is the first thought with which up to now every culture has come to consciousness of itself. A downpour of revelations, wonders and peerings into the primordial ground of things swamped every deeper mind. They thought, they lived, only in apocalyptic images. Reality became appearance. Strange and awesome sights were recounted from one to another, read out of confused and obscure scriptures and at once seized on with imme-

---

[1] *Der Untergang des Abendlandes: Umrisse einer Morphologie der Weltgeschichte*, Band II. *Welthistorische Perspectiven* (München, 1923, revised ed.), pp. 258ff. The work has now run into upwards of 50,000 copies, a proof of very widely extended serious interest, for it is not a 'popular' exposition. It may be stated that Spengler shows by his references that he is acquainted with the most recent Mandæan studies.

diate inner certainty. From one community to another, from village to village, wandered such writings, of which it is impossible to say that they belonged to any one single religion. They are Persian, Chaldæan, Jewish in colouring; but they have all taken up what was at that time circulating in men's minds. The canonical books are national; the apocalyptic are international and literally so. They come into existence without any appearing to be their authors. Their contents mingle and melt together; they read to-day one way and to-morrow another. But they are anything but poësy, fiction (*Dichtung*). They are like the fearsome figures round the doors of the Romance cathedrals in France, which also are no 'Art,' but Dread turned into stóne. Every man knew these angels and demons, these heaven-ascending and hell-descending numinous beings,—the Primal Man or Second Adam, the Messenger of God, the Saviour of the Last Day, the Son of Man, the Eternal City and the Final Judgment. In the foreign cities and in the high-seats of the powerful Persian and Jewish priesthood there had to be a conceptual fixation of distinctive doctrines; but here down among the folk there was hardly any particular religion, but rather a general 'magic' religiosity which filled all souls and fastened upon sights and shapes of every conceivable origin. The Last Day had drawn nigh. They expected it. They knew that 'he' must now be manifested, 'he' of whom all revelations spake. Prophets arose. People banded together into ever new associations and circles in the conviction of having now come to better knowledge of their native religion or of having found the true one. In this period of tremendous and yearly increasing tension, in the years hard by the birth of

Jesus, alongside numerous other communities and sects arose the Mandæan religion of salvation. Of its founder or origin we are in ignorance. In spite of its detestation of the Judaism of Jerusalem and its marked predilection for Persian settings of the notion of salvation, it nevertheless seems to have stood very near the popular belief of Syrian Jewry. Of its marvel-filled scriptures one piece after another now comes to light. 'He' is everywhere,—the Son of Man,[1] the Saviour sent into the deep, who must himself be saved, the goal of the expectation. In the John-Book the Father raised on high in the House of Perfection, surrounded with Light, speaks to his Only-begotten Son: My Son, be for me an Envoy—go unto the world of the Darkness, in which is no Light-ray. The Son cries on high: Father of Greatness, what sin have I done that thou hast sent me into the deep? And at the end: Without faults I ascended, and fault and defect were not in me.

"All the traits of the great prophetical religions and the whole treasury of the deepest insights and figures which have since been assembled in apocalyptic, lie here at the bottom in common. But of 'antique' (?=Hellenic) thinking and feeling not a breath has penetrated into this underworld of the 'magic.' The beginnings of the new religion are, it may well be, for ever lost to memory. But *one* historical figure of Mandaism comes on to the stage with arresting clearness, tragical in its striving and ending, like Jesus himself: it is John the Baptizer. Scarce still belonging to Jewry, and filled with strong detestation . . . of the spirit of Jerusalem, he proclaims the End of the

---

[1] The Mandæans do not use this idiom; it is ever simply the Man.—G. R. S. M.

World and the Coming of the Barnasha, the Son of Man, who is *no longer the promised national Messiah of the Jews, but the Bringer of the World-conflagration.* To him went Jesus and became one of his disciples. Jesus was thirty years old when the awakening came upon him. The apocalyptic and in particular the Mandæan thought-world from now on filled his whole consciousness. The other world of historic reality lay round him as in seeming only, strange and unmeaning. That 'he' will now come and put an end to this so unreal reality, was Jesus' great certainty, and for this certainty he came forward as announcer like John, his teacher. The oldest gospel-accounts taken into the New Testament still let some glimmer of this period shine through in which he was in his consciousness no more than a prophet." It was later that the conviction came upon him: Thou art thyself 'he.'

This is a boldly sketched outline bringing into special prominence the dominant eschatological feature of the picture, but with no indications of the particular Mandæan colouring or shading that must be used in the completed canvas. For this, however, we cannot reproach Spengler, seeing that we find ourselves compelled to refrain from any such attempt. And the reason for this abstention is quite simple. Lidzbarski's substantive and scientific translation of the John-Book and Liturgies enables the student at first-hand to become so exhaustively acquainted with this part of the material, that much in it reads differently, and the whole atmosphere savours differently from the general impression produced even by the most attentive perusal of Brandt's praiseworthy and painstaking pioneer labours. It seems therefore naturally to follow that, when we get the full translation of the remaining and earliest deposit, the *Genzā*, from Lidzbarski, and can then survey the whole of its matter in detail, and so review in their native settings and contexts the selected features of it sketched by Brandt and in reliance on him utilized by Bousset and Reitzenstein, for instance, we shall be enabled to appreciate the whole tradition more understandably and analyze it more accurately. We shall then be in a position to trace, for instance, the development of the meaning attached to the figure of the victor and of the formula 'the Man who has come hither,' and also the modifications of eschatological notions within the Mandæan scheme of reference and much else.

Meantime it is already evident that the Mandæan Nazōræan tradition preserves traces of doctrine and endeavour and other features of very great value for recovering long-lost indications of one of the most important backgrounds of Christian origins and of a subsequent parallel development of religious faith. In any case the study of the Mandæan documents cannot fail to come to the front as an indispensable task in the elucidation of the characteristic Gnosis as an integral and widely-diffused factor in the general history of religion in the critical centuries in the Near East and Mediterranean West before and after the beginnings of the present era. And this study, were it necessary where so much similar recent research has already made it certain on all hands, gives the final death-blow to the old misleading view that Gnosticism was of interest solely as a Christian heresy, and was to be evaluated as such and comfortably disposed of in the good old cavalier Patristic fashion.

It is pleasant to think that new light will be

thrown, directly or indirectly, on our subject by a number of important studies which are in hand or which have been already made public in lecture-form. Among them may be mentioned the Lectures on Manichæism by Prof. F. Crawford Burkitt and the long-expected work on the same religion by the veteran Iranist Prof. J. Williams Jackson, and also the arresting Schweich Lectures of this year on the Samaritans by Dr. Moses Gaster, whose researches into their little-known literature, based on his unique and famous collection of MSS. that has just been acquired by the British Museum, open up quite new vistas of O.T. study and also supply indications of a new and hitherto unsuspected background that may be brought into line with Mandæanism and hence with general Christian origins.

Printed in the United States
83219LV00006B/26/A